CONTEMPORARY
TURKISH POLITICS

CONTEMPORARY TURKISH POLITICS

Challenges to Democratic Consolidation

Ergun Özbudun

LYNNE
RIENNER
PUBLISHERS

BOULDER
LONDON

Published in the United States of America in 2000 by
Lynne Rienner Publishers, Inc.
1800 30th Street, Boulder, Colorado 80301
www.rienner.com

and in the United Kingdom by
Lynne Rienner Publishers, Inc.
3 Henrietta Street, Covent Garden, London WC2E 8LU

Library of Congress Cataloging-in-Publication Data
Özbudun, Ergun
    Contemporary Turkish politics :   challenges to democratic
  consolidation   /   by Ergun Özbudun.
      p.   cm.
    Includes bibliographical references (p.   ) and index.
    ISBN 1-55587-735-4 (alk. paper)
    1. Turkey—Politics and government—20th century.   I. Title.
JQ1805.A7092   1999
320.9561'09'045—dc21   99-38717
                                                           CIP

British Cataloguing in Publication Data
A Cataloguing in Publication record for this book
is available from the British Library.

Printed and bound in the United States of America

The paper used in this publication meets the requirements
∞ of the American National Standard for Permanence of
Paper for Printed Library Materials Z39.48-1984.

5 4   3   2   1

To Umay

Contents

Acknowledgments

This book grew out of my lectures on contemporary Turkish politics at Bilkent University, Ankara. I owe a great deal to my colleagues and students for providing intellectual stimulation. I am also grateful to the anonymous reviewers at Lynne Rienner Publishers for their constructive comments and criticism, as well as to the Turkish Academy of Sciences for providing financial assistance for my research. Warm thanks go to Isıl Üzümcü, who typed several versions of the manuscript. Last but not least, I am grateful to my wife, Umay Özbudun, to whom this book is dedicated, whose patience and constant encouragement provided invaluable support in this endeavor.

1

Introduction

The literature on democratization published since the mid-1970s, particularly on transitions to and the consolidation of democracy, can easily fill a library. This book grew out of my belief that Turkey is an interesting test case for many recent theories on democratization. Indeed, Turkey is not a "third-wave" but a "second-wave" democracy, having made a transition to democracy in the late 1940s. Thus, it has a fairly long history of democratic politics. Yet Turkish democracy has been interrupted three times by military interventions: it has experienced three democratic breakdowns and three restorations of democracy. Today, Turkey is still far from having reached the level of advanced representative democracies; why this is the case is the fundamental question that this book addresses.

Turkey is an interesting test case also because it is the only democratic and truly secular country in the Islamic world. In view of recent debates on the compatibility of Islam and democracy, the Turkish example is certainly worth studying; the success or failure of Turkey's democratic experiment will tell us much about such compatibility. In this book, the challenge to the secular state posed by the rising trend of political Islam is analyzed in some depth.

Another reason I was encouraged to write this book is the significant absence of a comparative dimension in Turkish studies. Interestingly, Turkey occupies no place in comparative Middle Eastern studies or in comparative southern European studies. Comparative works on Middle Eastern political systems have almost always concentrated on Arab countries, sometimes adding Iran. Recent studies on the three new democracies in southern Europe (Spain, Portugal, and Greece) have not as a rule included Turkey in their comparative analyses.[1] Comparisons with Latin American countries, with which Turkey shares many important characteristics, are almost totally absent.[2] Although this book is not systematically comparative, in many places comparisons are made with the experiences of other new democracies.

Because this study is about the consolidation of democracy in Turkey and the challenges it faces, I will start with a definition of democratic consolidation. Aptly, Adam Przeworski describes it as a situation in which democracy "becomes the only game in town, when no one can imagine acting outside democratic institutions, when all the losers want to do is to try again within the same institutions under which they have just lost. Democracy is consolidated when it becomes self-enforcing, that is, when all the relevant political forces find it best to continue to submit their interests and values to the uncertain interplay of the institutions."[3]

Defining democratic consolidation involves making a choice between the maximalist and the minimalist notions of consolidation. A maximalist definition would emphasize the inculcation of democratic values among the majority of citizens through a long socialization process; a minimalist definition would stress the absence of significant challenges to the legitimacy of democratic institutions and particularly the prevalence of free and competitive elections.[4] Problems are involved in both approaches. For example, if the maximalist approach is carried to the extreme, no democratic regime can be considered truly consolidated. Also, this approach does not square with historical realities because "in no known case does there appear to have been a majority of democrats before the advent of political democracy."[5]

The minimalist approach, on the other hand, runs the risk of "electoralism," or equating democratic consolidation simply with holding regular competitive elections. This approach carries two important caveats. One involves the tutelary powers and reserved domains of nonelected authorities, particularly the military: "In some instances it is possible that democratically elected governments may succeed one another for a considerable time without reversals simply as a result of the caution of [their] leadership in not challenging actors whose power escapes democratic accountability. In this case the resulting stability cannot be equated with progress towards creating a fully democratic regime."[6] The second caveat concerns the degree to which basic civil liberties are respected. This dimension is as important as the prevalence of competitive elections "because a regime can hold competitive elections with broad participation, yet in the absence of guarantees of civil liberties, it is not fully democratic."[7] Thus, even a minimal procedural notion of democratic consolidation must include the superiority of democratically elected civilian authorities over nonelected ones, as well as broad respect and effective guarantees for the basic civil liberties of all citizens.

In the sense defined here, the notion of consolidation seems to have much in common with that of political institutionalization—a situation in which the formal and informal rules of the regime are widely understood and accepted and the major political actors pattern their behavior accordingly.[8] This identification is correct, however, only to the extent that the institutionalized patterns of behavior are truly democratic. If they are not—for example, when nonelected authorities enjoy wide tutelary powers or reserved policy domains, or the basic rights of some sections of the population are not effectively respected—institutionalization may have a "perverse" character, that is, it will not lead to democratic consolidation but will detract from it.[9] In short, political institutionalization must be seen as only one, albeit an important, ingredient of democratic consolidation. By the same token, the "two-turnover test" proposed by Samuel Huntington cannot be taken as a conclusive criterion of democratic consolidation.[10] Besides, this test is more meaningful in presidential and two-party parliamentary situations than in multiparty parliamentary systems where frequent changes in government do not necessarily lead to democratic consolidation. In Turkey between 1973 and 1980, three turnovers occurred between the governments led by Bülent Ecevit and Süleyman Demirel without contributing at all to democratic consolidation, as was amply shown by the collapse of democracy in 1980.

This discussion suggests that a large gray area exists between the moment of completed democratic transition and that of democratic consolidation. Here Guillermo O'Donnell's notion of "two transitions" is particularly useful. O'Donnell argues that conceptualizing the process of democratization implies two transitions:

> The first is the transition from the previous authoritarian regime to the installation of a democratic government. The second transition is from this government to the consolidation of democracy, or, in other words, to the effective functioning of a *democratic regime*. . . . The second transition will not be any less arduous nor any less lengthy; the paths that lead from a democratic government to a democratic regime are uncertain and complex, and the possibilities of authoritarian regression are numerous.[11]

The difficulties of the second transition mean that many of the new democracies lie within this gray area, ranging from *democraduras* to more or less functioning but still not fully consolidated democracies—a fate Turkey shares with many other countries.

In this book, I have adopted Juan J. Linz and Alfred Stepan's definition of democratic consolidation as one that avoids the drawbacks of both the maximalist and minimalist approaches. The authors define democratic consolidation in behavioral, attitudinal, and constitutional terms:

> Behaviorally, a democratic regime in a territory is consolidated when no significant national, social, economic, political, or institutional actors spend significant resources attempting to achieve their objectives by creating a nondemocratic regime or turning to violence or foreign intervention to secede from the state.
>
> Attitudinally, a democratic regime is consolidated when a strong majority of public opinion holds the belief that democratic procedures and institutions are the most appropriate way to govern collective life in a society such as theirs and when the support for antisystem alternatives is quite small or more or less isolated from the pro-democratic forces.
>
> Constitutionally, a democratic regime is consolidated when governmental and nongovernmental forces alike, throughout the territory of the state, become subjected to, and habituated to, the resolution of conflict within the specific laws, procedures, and institutions sanctioned by the new democratic process.[12]

Linz and Stepan argue that in addition to a functioning state, which is a sine qua non of a consolidated democracy, five other interconnected and mutually reinforcing conditions must also exist or be crafted for a democracy to be consolidated. First, the conditions must exist for the development of a free and lively civil society. Second, there must be a relatively autonomous and valued political society. Third, there must be a rule of law to ensure legal guarantees for citizens' freedoms and independent associational life. Fourth, there must be a state bureaucracy that is usable by the new democratic government. Fifth, there must be an institutionalized economic society.[13]

In all five arenas of democratic consolidation, Turkey presents some characteristics that are likely to facilitate consolidation and others that are likely to impede it. With regard to a functioning state, from Ottoman times to the present Turkey has enjoyed a remarkably high degree of "stateness" and a strong state tradition.[14] Yet since the mid-1980s such stateness has been challenged by a relatively small but militant and violent group of Kurdish secessionists organized under the banner of the Kurdistan Workers' Party (PKK).

With regard to the existence of a free and lively civil society, Turkey holds a comparative advantage over postcommunist democracies. Turkey has no totalitarian past. The single-party regime of the Republican People's Party (RPP) that ruled Turkey from 1923 to 1946 was an authoritarian rather than a totalitarian regime; therefore, it permitted limited pluralism and did not attempt to suppress all expressions of civil society in the nonpolitical arena. At the same time, however, voluntary associations were subject to a highly illiberal law that, among other things, prohibited the establishment of class-based associations. Also, in the early 1930s many leading voluntary associations were induced to "voluntarily" dissolve themselves. Civil society institutions showed steady growth after the transition to democracy in 1946 and received a particularly strong boost with the adoption of the liberal 1961 constitution. They faced a serious setback, however, during the period of military rule by the National Security Council (NSC). The 1982 constitution adopted by the NSC banned all kinds of political activities by civil institutions except for political parties, and it prohibited cooperation between political parties and such institutions as trade unions, voluntary associations, foundations, and professional organizations. These illiberal provisions of the constitution were repealed by the 1995 constitutional amendment, but the numbers and activities of civil society organizations had grown rapidly in the 1980s and 1990s, forcing the limits of legal restrictions. Today, civil society has become an important element in the political discourse. Under the best of conditions, however, civil organizations have yet to contend with a strong state tradition and an exceedingly centralized decision-making mechanism with little input from such organizations.

With regard to a political society, Turkey has had more than half a century of experience with multiparty politics, not including the earlier and shorter experiments in the last decades of the Ottoman Empire and the first years of the republic. Huntington argues that "prior democratic experience is more conducive than none to the stabilization of third wave democracies. Extending this proposition it may also be reasonable to hypothesize that a longer and more recent experience with democracy is more conducive to democratic consolidation than is a shorter and more distant one."[15] By these criteria, Turkey's long democratic experience, although thrice interrupted, can be considered a facilitating condition for democratic consolidation. Technically, Turkey is not a third-wave but a second-wave democracy. And yet, as analyzed in Chapter 4, the Turkish party system currently faces serious problems of volatility, fragmentation, polarization, and an overall decline in the organizational strength of political parties.

Turkey holds a comparative advantage over many new democracies in having a relatively long tradition of constitutionalism and the rule of law. The origins of the rule-of-law tradition go back to the Imperial Edict of 1839, which established guarantees for the life, honor, and property of the sultan's subjects and recognized equality for all subjects before the law regardless of religion. The Ottoman Empire was also the first Muslim state to proclaim a constitution—in 1876—with a partially elected legislative assembly. Although the constitution was suspended in 1878, it was restored in 1908 and remained in force until the end of the Ottoman Empire. Even during the single-party years, the appearance of a constitutional government was carefully preserved, and extraordinary courts were established only during acute emergencies. One-party elections were held regularly, and the legislature (the Turkish Grand National Assembly) was held in high esteem, even though in practice it normally limited itself to rubber stamping decisions of top party leaders. The Republican constitutions of 1961 and 1982 established a strong and independent Constitutional Court, recognized the independence of the judiciary, and provided tenure and secure income for all judges and public prosecutors. All personnel and disciplinary decisions regarding judges and public prosecutors are made by the Supreme Council of Judges and Public Prosecutors, composed primarily of judges nominated by the higher courts and appointed by the president. The Turkish judicial system is not without problems. The slow working of the courts gives rise to legitimate complaints and sometimes encourages Mafia-type extrajudicial solutions. The European Court of Human Rights has decided that the State Security Courts (mixed courts composed of civilian and military judges and competent to try cases involving crimes against state security) do not conform with European standards of the rule of law. Last but not least, frequent allegations have been made of police torture and mistreatment, which usually go unpunished.

With regard to a "usable" state bureaucracy, the Turkish Republic inherited from the Ottoman Empire a strong and centralized, highly bureaucratic state in which rational-legal bureaucratic norms prevail. Indeed, the "output" structures of the state—such as the public bureaucracy, the armed forces, the police, and the courts—have been so highly institutionalized that this overdevelopment of the state machinery, coupled with the predominance of a strong state tradition in Turkish political culture, may impede the emergence of more balanced patterns of state–civil society relationships. One can argue that not only the lack of political institutionalization but also overinstitutionalization of the state machinery, coupled with weak institutionalization of the input structures (political parties and interest groups), may constrain prospects for democratic consolidation.[16]

Finally, with regard to the existence of an "economic society," Turkey again holds a comparative advantage over postcommunist democracies. Linz and Stepan, arguing that there has been no modern consolidated democracy in either a command economy or a pure market economy, conclude that "modern consolidated democracies require a set of socio-politically crafted and socio-politically accepted norms, institutions, and regulations, which we call *economic* society, that mediates between state and market." Even under the most liberal market conditions, "markets require corporation laws; the regulation of stock markets; regulated standards for weight, measurement, and ingredients; and the protection of property, both public and private. All of these require a role for the state in the economy."[17] The Turkish economy has always been a mixed economy with a large public sector together with private enterprises; thus, an economic society has long existed in Turkey. The "statism" of the single-party regime (1923–1946) was not an antibusiness ideology but simply meant state initiative in industrialization, especially in areas where private capital was either insufficient or reluctant to invest. The private sector grew steadily after the transition to democracy, and in the 1980s important steps were taken to increase the role of market forces in the conduct of the economy. Still, the state plays a predominant role in making economic policies, with relatively little input from the private sector, and this has had a negative impact on the growth of civil society, as is discussed in Chapter 6.

Turning now to an outline of the chapters that follow, Chapter 2 analyzes Turkey's three transitions (or retransitions) to democracy and the three corresponding breakdowns. The first transition from the well-established single-party authoritarian regime of the RPP took place between 1946 and 1950, ending with the opposition Democratic Party's (DP) victory in the free popular elections of 14 May 1950. Under DP rule, relations between the government and the RPP opposition quickly deteriorated, as the DP government increasingly resorted to authoritarian measures after 1954. The ten-year DP rule came to an end with the military intervention of 27 May 1960. The ruling military council (the National Unity Committee) prepared a new democratic constitution in collaboration with the opposition political parties and supervised conditions for the retransition to democracy with the parliamentary elections in October 1961.

Turkey's second try at democracy was interrupted in March 1971 by a "coup by memorandum," which forced the government to resign and replaced it with a so-called above party, or technocratic government. The 1971 intervention, however, neither dissolved the parliament nor banned political parties. This interim period ended with parliamentary elections in 1973. The post-1973 period was increasingly marked by intense political polarization and large-scale acts of political violence perpetrated by groups on the extreme left and extreme right. The military intervention of 12 September 1980 ended this chaotic situation and started a new period of military rule, that of the NSC. The NSC rule came to an end with the parliamentary elections of November 1983, under conditions carefully controlled by the outgoing government.

One of the main arguments in Chapter 2 is that all three transitions to democracy in Turkey (1950, 1961, and 1983) displayed the essential characteristics of the reform mode of transition—in which the transition process was initiated and controlled by the authoritarian power holders—with important consequences for the ensuing democratic regimes. Another central argument of the chapter is that the most powerful explanatory variable for the three democratic breakdowns (particularly those in 1960 and 1980) was the behavior of the political elites: that is, intense elite polarization and the intransigent attitudes of mainstream politicians.

Chapter 3 is devoted to an analysis of the constitution-making processes following the 1960 and 1980 military interventions. These processes provide a perspective on the balance of political forces in the aftermath of the military interventions and on relations between the military and civilian political forces. Also, the mode of constitution making clearly affects the nature of the outcome (the constitutions) and has important consequences for the newly emerging democratic regime. Thus, I argue that the exclusionary or quasi-exclusionary nature of the constitution-making processes (the first excluded former Democrats, and the second excluded all political parties) adversely affected the stability of the ensuing democratic regimes, thus depriving the constitutions of popular legitimacy.

Political parties and the party system are the subjects of Chapter 4. Since the first transition to democracy in 1950, Turkish politics have largely been party politics. The two-party system of the 1946–1960 period was transformed into a multiparty system following the 1960 military intervention, in part as a result of the adoption of a proportional representation system and in part as a reflection of the growing complexity and differentiation of the society. The last years of Turkey's second try at democracy were increasingly marked by growing volatility, fragmentation, and polarization of the party system, which with other factors contributed to the breakdown of democracy in 1980. The NSC regime attempted to restructure the party system by introducing high national- and constituency-level thresholds in hopes that the more ideological minor parties would be eliminated from competition and a two-party (or at least a three-party) system would be established. The 1983 and 1987 elections did produce a single-party government (the Motherland Party). The party system began to fragment again in 1987, however, and today it is as volatile, fragmented, and polarized as ever, with little hope of stabilization in the near future.

Chapter 4 also analyzes the general organizational characteristics of Turkish political parties and the main features of the principal individual parties. There is special emphasis on the Welfare Party (WP), which represents the rising challenge of political Islam.

Chapter 5 addresses another major actor in Turkish politics, the military. Since 1960, not only has the military directly intervened three times, but it also has played a major political role during the civilian governments that followed the periods of military rule. The military's political influence has been aided and enhanced by the "exit guarantees" the outgoing military regimes obtained in the 1961 and 1982 constitutions. Such guarantees assure the military of an important share of political power by giving it certain tutelary powers, reserved policy domains, and great autonomy vis-à-vis civilian governments, and this feature of Turkish politics is one of the constraining factors for the further consolidation of democracy.

Chapter 6 discusses the growth of civil society and its influence on policymaking, with particular emphasis on the relationship among business interests, political leadership, and the state apparatus. Here, I examine the extent to which civil society is able to hold the government accountable. Also considered in this chapter are two new challenges to consolidation—the rise of political Islam and that of Kurdish nationalism—that are derived from the dynamics of civil society. Both challenges threaten some of the basic characteristics of the Turkish state, namely, its secular, national, and unitary nature. Elite congruence on these two issues seems extremely unlikely because it would involve a fundamental redefinition of the very nature of the Turkish state as it existed since the founding of the republic.

In conclusion, Chapter 7 presents a balance sheet for the consolidation of democracy in Turkey and also discusses Turkey's place among the new democracies. How does Turkey fit in with other case studies? What are the similarities and differences? Is a new type of democracy needed to explain the Turkish case? In this last regard, I explore whether Guillermo O'Donnell's notion of "delegative democracy" can be applied to Turkey. O'Donnell's model, developed on the basis of the Latin American experience, refers to a democracy that is neither consolidated (institutionalized) nor prone to the danger of imminent collapse. Its chief characteristics are an extremely personalistic style of leadership, weak political institutions (particularly political parties), and the lack of horizontal accountability (i.e., accountability to other autonomous institutions such as legislatures and the courts).[18] I argue that Turkey does share some important characteristics with the delegative democracies of Latin America.

NOTES

1. One exception is Ulrike Liebert and Maurizio Cotta, eds., *Parliament and Democratic Consolidation in Southern Europe: Greece, Italy, Portugal, Spain, and Turkey* (London: Pinter, 1990).

2. Again, an exception is Ergun Özbudun, "Established Revolution Versus Unfinished Revolution: Contrasting Patterns of Democratization in Mexico and Turkey," in Samuel P. Huntington and Clement H. Moore, eds., *Authoritarian Politics in Modern Society: The Dynamics of Established One-Party Systems* (New York: Basic Books, 1970), 380–405.

3. Adam Przeworski, *Democracy and the Market: Political and Economic Reforms in Eastern Europe and Latin America* (Cambridge: Cambridge University Press, 1991), 26.

4. Guillermo O'Donnell, "Transitions, Continuities, and Paradoxes," in Scott Mainwaring, Guillermo O'Donnell, and J. Samuel Valenzuela, eds., *Issues in Democratic Consolidation: The New South American Democracies in Comparative Perspective* (Notre Dame: University of Notre Dame Press, 1992), 48–49.

5. Ibid, 19–20. See also Samuel P. Huntington, "Will More Countries Become Democratic?" *Political Science Quarterly* 99 (summer 1984): 212. Dankwart A. Rustow was one of the first scholars who observed that to promote democracy one did not first need to foster Democrats. See his "Transitions to Democracy: Toward a Dynamic Model," *Comparative Politics* 2 (April 1970): 337–363.

6. J. Samuel Valenzuela, "Democratic Consolidation in Post-Transitional Settings: Notion, Process, and Facilitating Conditions," in Scott Mainwaring, Guillermo O'Donnell, and J. Samuel Valenzuela, eds., *Issues in Democratic Consolidation: The New South American Democracies in Comparative Perspective* (Notre Dame: University of Notre Dame Press, 1992), 59.

7. Scott Mainwaring, "Transitions to Democracy and Democratic Consolidation: Theoretical and Comparative Issues," in Scott

Mainwaring, Guillermo O'Donnell, and J. Samuel Valenzuela, eds., *Issues in Democratic Consolidation: The New South American Democracies in Comparative Perspective* (Notre Dame: University of Notre Dame Press, 1992), 298.

8. Ibid., 296.

9. Valenzuela, "Democratic Consolidation in Post-Transitional Settings," 68–70.

10. Samuel P. Huntington, *The Third Wave: Democratization in the Late Twentieth Century* (Norman: University of Oklahoma Press, 1991), 266–267.

11. O'Donnell, "Transitions, Continuities, and Paradoxes," 18–19.

12. Juan J. Linz and Alfred Stepan, *Problems of Democratic Transition and Consolidation: Southern Europe, South America, and Post-Communist Europe* (Baltimore: Johns Hopkins University Press, 1996), 6.

13. Ibid., 7.

14. Metin Heper, *The State Tradition in Turkey* (Walkington: Eothen, 1985); Ergun Özbudun, "The Ottoman Legacy and the Middle East State Tradition," in L. Carl Brown, ed., *Imperial Legacy: The Ottoman Imprint on the Balkans and the Middle East* (New York: Columbia University Press, 1996), 133–157.

15. Huntington, *The Third Wave*, 270–271. Cf. Adam Przeworski, Michael Alvarez, José Antonio Cheibub, and Fernando Limogni, "What Makes Democracies Endure?" *Journal of Democracy* 7 (January 1996): 43–44.

16. Metin Heper, "Strong State as a Problem for the Consolidation of Democracy: Turkey and Germany Compared," *Comparative Political Studies* 25 (July 1992): 169–194.

17. Linz and Stepan, *Problems of Democratic Transition and Consolidation*, 11–12.

18. Guillermo O'Donnell, "Delegative Democracy," *Journal of Democracy* 5 (January 1994): 55–69.

2

Democratic Transitions, Breakdowns, and Restorations in Comparative Perspective

Since around 1945, Turkish political history can be recounted in terms of such concepts as regime changes, democratic transitions, crises, breakdowns, and restorations. Excluding its first competitive but controversial elections in 1946, Turkey, a second-wave democracy,[1] had twelve free and competitive general elections for its national parliament during this period—as well as three military interruptions of the democratic process. Each time the military intervened—in 1960, 1971, and 1980—democracy was restored relatively quickly and smoothly, suggesting that the soldiers' intention on each occasion was a moderating coup rather than the creation of a lasting military regime.

Yet few analysts would call Turkey a stable or consolidated democracy. The continuing elusiveness of consolidation, despite half a century of multiparty politics, indicates a certain malaise and makes Turkey an interesting case for comparative purposes. Thus, this chapter analyzes regime changes in Turkey in light of recent theoretical and comparative perspectives. Put differently, Turkey is used as a test case for the hypotheses put forward in comparative research regarding regime changes and transitions.

DEMOCRATIC TRANSITIONS

Transition from Single-Party Rule (1945–1950)

Of the three transitions to democracy in the period under study (in 1945, 1961, and 1983), the first is the most important for theoretical and practical reasons because it involved the end of an established and enduring single-party regime (the Republican People's Party [RPP]) that lasted more than twenty years.[2] This transition from authoritarianism to competitive politics is highly exceptional in that it took place without a *ruptura* (a sudden break with existing institutional arrangements). On the contrary, it was a good example of *reforma*, in which the transition process was led and controlled by the power holders of the previous authoritarian regime.

Signs of liberalization of RPP rule started to appear in 1944, although some traces could be found earlier. Ismet Inönü, president of the republic and leader of the RPP, encouraged the new mood in his address to the National Assembly on 1 November 1944, saying that "our government is a popular government in the fullest sense. This government has been developing democratic principles in accordance with Turkey's structure and her special conditions."[3] Much stronger encouragement came on 19 May 1945, when Inönü stated:

> The political regime and the government of the people established by the Republican regime shall develop in all aspects and in every way, and as the conditions imposed by war disappear, democratic principles will gradually acquire a larger place in the political and cultural life of the country. The Grand National Assembly, our greatest democratic institution, had the Government in its hand from the very beginning and constantly developed the country in the direction of democracy.[4]

In May and June 1945, intense and heated debates occurred in the Assembly on the land reform bill proposed by the government—the first genuine and protracted controversy in the normally docile single-party Assembly in two decades. Indeed, the bill was saved only by Inönü's personal intervention. At about the same time, four RPP deputies who were among the leaders of the opposition to the land reform bill submitted a proposal demanding in rather general terms that the party constitution and some laws be modified in accordance with democratic principles. The proposal was rejected by the RPP parliamentary group; when the four signatories continued to voice their criticism in the press, three were expelled from the party, and the fourth, Celal Bayar, resigned from both the party and his Assembly seat.

Inönü's Assembly speech on 1 November 1945 was considered a definite green light for further democratization. He said, in fact:

> The democratic character has been preserved in principle throughout the Republican period. Dictatorship, in principle, has never been accepted and it has been considered harmful and unbecoming to [the] Turkish nation. Our only shortcoming is the absence of a party to face the government party. There have been past experiences in this direction. There have even been attempts encouraged by those in power. It is unfortunate that such attempts failed twice because of the reactions that appeared in the country. But the needs of the country will lead to the establishment of another political party through the normal operation of the atmosphere of freedom and democracy.

Inönü further encouraged the dissidents within the RPP to come into the open instead of working as a faction within the party.[5]

Soon after this encouraging statement, on 7 January 1946, the four signatories of the proposal mentioned earlier officially formed the Democratic Party (DP) under the leadership of Celal Bayar. Bayar submitted the DP program to Inönü for his approval before it was officially submitted to the government. Inönü made it clear that he was sensitive on three points: preservation of the secular character of the state, foreign policy, and the campaign to spread primary education.[6] In fact, by that time another opposition party had been formed by Nuri Demirag, a rich industrialist, who on 18 July 1945 founded the National Development Party. The new party attracted little attention, "but by allowing its establishment, the government proved its willingness to accept opposition parties."[7]

In the following months, local DP organizations spread rapidly throughout the country. The RPP Congress convened on 10 May 1946 to make changes in the party constitution to adapt itself to the new circumstances of political competition. Congress decided to propose laws lifting the ban on the formation of associations and political parties based on class interest; to adopt direct voting in place of the old indirect (two-stage) voting; to make the party chair elective instead of good for a lifetime; to abolish the Independent Group, which had lost its raison d'être because of the emergence of a true opposition party; and to hold the next Assembly elections in 1946 instead of at their regular time in 1947.[8]

The first truly competitive elections in Turkish history took place on 21 July 1946; after a vigorous campaign the DP won 62 seats as opposed to 396 for the RPP, with 7 seats for independents.[9] The Democrats claimed large-scale electoral fraud and manipulation had been committed, the true extent of which seems difficult to establish. As a result of this controversy, further democratization of the electoral process remained a principal demand of the DP in the 1946–1950 period.

Although the 1946 elections, controversial though they were, were an important step in democratization, the rest of the transition process was neither sudden nor smooth. The old guard of the RPP—led by Recep Peker, who was prime minister from August 1946 to September 1947—was not anxious to remove restrictions on opposition activities. At most, Peker would have tolerated a much more gradual transition. The so-called extremists within the DP, on the other hand, did not trust the intentions of the government and advocated withdrawal from the Assembly to concentrate on propaganda work among the people (*sine-i millete dönmek*). To many in the RPP, such a course looked dangerously like seditious activity. In the end, both parties managed to pursue moderate policies, which significantly contributed to the success of the transition, as is analyzed further later.

Inönü's firm commitment to democracy was perhaps the most important factor in the transition process. Indeed, whenever relations between the government and the opposition grew tense, he intervened personally to soften the atmosphere and reassure the opposition. The most significant intervention was his statement on 12 July 1947 (known as the 12 July Declaration), following several rounds of talks with Prime Minister Peker and opposition leader Bayar, in which he said:

> An opposition party which uses legal methods and not revolutionary ones must enjoy the same privileges as the party in power. On this ground I consider myself, as the head of the

state, equally responsible to both parties. . . . The responsibility of the government to maintain law and order is a fact, but its impartial attitude towards all the political parties established legally is the basic guarantee for political life. . . . The opposition will work in a security without fearing the party in power. The Administration will consider that the opposition demands only the rights legally conferred upon it, while the citizens at large will view with confidence and tranquillity the possibility of having the government powers in the hands of one or the other party. The obstacles to this end are mainly psychological and in order to overcome them I should like to ask the genuine cooperation of the leaders of the opposition and the government.[10]

The 12 July Declaration was a turning point in the transition process. Shortly afterward, Peker resigned from the premiership because of his differences with Inönü and in the face of increasing opposition from a moderate or liberal group within the RPP (called the "Thirty-Fives"). Peker was replaced as premier by the more moderate Hasan Saka on 10 September 1947. Peker's final challenge to Inönü at the Seventh Congress of the RPP (17 November–4 December 1947) failed decisively; he mustered only 25 votes for the party leadership against 595 for Inönü.[11] Saka's cabinet gave way to that of Semseddin Günaltay on 16 January 1949. The Günaltay government was dominated by liberals, and the final obstacles to a smooth transition were removed during his premiership. Most notably, the electoral law was changed in February 1950 (law number 5545), incorporating most of the demands put forward by the Democrats. The new law introduced secret voting, as well as open counting and sorting of ballots; it also established a system of judicial supervision of electoral administration, although the final say regarding the invalidation of elections or the credentials of an individual deputy remained with the Grand National Assembly. In the elections of 14 May 1950, held under the new law, the Democrats won 53.3 percent of the popular vote and 408 seats (83.8 percent) in the Assembly versus 39.9 percent of the vote and 69 seats (14.2 percent) for the Republicans. Thus, the transition process ended with the peaceful transfer of power to the opposition.

The democratization process in Turkey between 1945 and 1950 clearly conforms to the reform mode of democratic transitions.[12] The transition process was initiated and carefully controlled by the power holders of the existing authoritarian regime;

it involved no element of a *ruptura*. On the contrary, the transition was accomplished without violence and within the constitutional rules of the old regime, to the extent that not a word of the 1924 constitution was changed. This may have resulted from the essentially democratic character of the constitution, which was adopted before the consolidation of the Kemalist regime and bore no trace of authoritarianism. Legal changes required by liberalization remained limited to the relatively minor ones mentioned earlier. Further, the Turkish transition displayed no characteristics of a pacted transition (*pactada*), which involves a more or less formal, binding agreement between the leaders of the government and those of the opposition regarding the conditions of the transition and the fundamental principles of the regime to be established. Therefore, pacts are generally seen when a rough equality of power exists between the government and the opposition. In the Turkish transition of 1946 to 1950, the DP opposition lacked the power to force the government into a negotiated pact; the government, with the support of the military and the entire state apparatus, was able to control every phase of the transition. The only aspect of the transition that bore some resemblance to a pact was the agreement on the 1950 electoral law. Thus, the Turkish case supports the hypothesis that democratic transitions through a reform path are possible only when the government is stronger than the opposition.

Another hypothesis supported by the Turkish case is that a transition by way of reform is possible only when the moderates (soft-liners) are stronger than the extremists (hard-liners) in both camps. Samuel P. Huntington has argued that "if standpatters dominated the government and extremists the opposition, democratization was impossible. . . . In transformations [reform mode], the interaction between reformers and standpatters within the governing coalition was of central importance; and the transformation only occurred if reformers were stronger than standpatters, if the government was stronger than the opposition, and if the moderates were stronger than the extremists."[13] Indeed, such a confrontation between moderates and extremists is observed in most democratic transitions, and the Turkish case neatly conforms to the rule. The hard-liners in the RPP were represented by Prime Minister Peker (1946–1947) and his followers; İnönü led the moderates. In the opposition camp, Bayar and his close colleagues represented the moderates; the extremists finally left the DP in 1948 and formed a new party, the Nation Party (NP). The NP leaders pursued a more uncompromising line vis-à-vis the government and labeled the DP *muvazaa partisi* (a party of collusion).[14] In the 1950 elections, the NP obtained only 3 percent of the votes and won only one seat in the National Assembly.

The moderation of the DP leadership was one of the most important factors in the successful completion of the transition process. The RPP government perceived the DP leadership not as a counterelite that would threaten the Kemalist legacy but as part of the Kemalist elite. Bayar was a close associate of Atatürk, his minister of economy for many years and his last prime minister. Other leading DP figures (including Adnan Menderes, Fuat Köprülü, and Refik Koraltan) were longtime RPP deputies. Marshal Fevzi Çakmak, the DP candidate for president of the republic in 1946, was another close friend of Atatürk's and was chief of the general staff during almost the entire Republican period. Columnist Falih Rıfkı Atay of the RPP daily *Ulus* described how the new opposition party was perceived by the government: "We wish success to Celal Bayar in establishing an opposition party loyal to the cause of Kemalism and to the traditions of the Turkish Revolution. Celal Bayar has earned a reputation in our party on account of his virtue, honesty, and idealism. Is it possible not to be happy if a leader of his qualifications forms an opposition party to face us?"[15]

The reform mode often involves at least a tacit understanding between the government reformers and moderates in the opposition.[16] It is noteworthy that despite its dominant position, the RPP government made no attempt to secure exit guarantees or a guaranteed share of power for itself in the coming democratic regime. This may have resulted from its leaders' confidence that they would easily win the 1950 elections. Thus, the Turkish case also supports the observation that miscalculations by government leaders often play an important role in democratic transitions. The 1950 Turkish elections provide a good example of Huntington's category of "stunning elections."[17]

Opinions vary as to the motives that led Inönü to initiate the reform process. Three factors are often mentioned: the international setting, socioeconomic transformations in Turkish society, and the nature of the existing authoritarian regime. With regard to the first, it is argued that the victory of democratic regimes in World War II and Turkey's need for a rapprochement with the West in the face of the Soviet threat provided the crucial incentive for reform.[18] Bernard Lewis, an eminent British historian of modern Turkey, argues, however, that

> there is . . . no evidence supporting the theory of direct American action in favor of political change. The most that can be said is that they [international factors] helped to create a favorable atmosphere. . . . The rulers of Turkey were not likely to change their form of government and surrender power to an opposition, merely to please a foreign state. And, if they did not know it from the start, they must soon have realized that the extension or restriction of democratic liberties in Turkey would have only a limited influence on a decision in Washington to help or abandon them.[19]

Feroz Ahmad concurs, saying that "America's principal concern was with regional and internal stability and not with democracy or multi-party politics." Necmeddin Sadak, who soon became foreign minister, "had spoken to the most influential American and British statesmen and that was their view. The stability of the Middle East was of vital importance and they did not object to the character of the regime so long as it was strong. They were even anxious lest party politics weaken Turkey."[20]

Other scholars associate the Turkish transition with structural changes that took place in society during the RPP rule. Thus, it has been argued that the RPP's etatism, far from being an antibusiness ideology, actually benefited the commercial and industrial sectors by creating an infrastructure, providing cheap intermediary goods, and training the cadres that later assumed managerial positions in the private sector. Consequently, the argument goes, "up to a point the bureaucracy and the commercial classes were able to get along together, but beyond that point the unity of interests broke down. By the end of World War II during which its wealth had increased by leaps and bounds, the bourgeoisie ceased to depend on the protection of the state—in fact, the protections had turned into fetters. . . . The commercial classes were convinced that their security would only be assured by the replacement of the bureaucrats."[21]

Little empirical evidence, however, shows that whatever domestic pressures might have existed at the time, they had reached such proportions that they forced the RPP leadership into this decision. Turkish society *had* reached a somewhat higher level of social differentiation and complexity by the end of single-party rule, but the RPP had other options, such as broadening its elite recruitment base to include pro-business groups or mobilizing poor peasants with the help of land reform. The experience of the Mexican Institutional Revolutionary Party suggests that a pragmatic single party can show sufficient adaptability to accommodate newly emerging groups. Although the DP's program included promises of economic liberalization, its real battle cry throughout its opposition years was political democracy—free and honest elections, extensive civil liberties, an end to arbitrary and authoritarian rule, and reduced power of the state bureaucracy. These issues were emphasized by the DP opposition to such an extent that the word *democracy* became almost magic in those years, a panacea for all ills.[22] This libertarian, antiauthoritarian, antibureaucratic outlook, rather than promises of economic liberalization, was what gave the DP its mass appeal and a broad but socially heterogeneous mass following.

Consequently, the main reasons for the Turkish transition should be sought in the nature of the RPP authoritarian regime. Ideological and organizational characteristics of the RPP made the transition an expected culmination of Kemalist reforms. The Turkish single-party regime remained closer to the liberal democratic tradition, both ideologically and organizationally, than to communist and fascist single-party regimes. The RPP had a positivist-rationalist "mentality" rather than an ideology.[23] This spirit was forcefully expressed by Atatürk: "The torch the Turkish nation holds in her hand and in her mind on her road to progress is positive science. . . . In the world, the truest guide for everything, for civilization, for life, for success is science. It is foolish to look for guidance outside the realm of science."[24] Kemalist principles grew out of action and in response to concrete needs and situations. As Dankwart A. Rustow observed, Kemal Atatürk "displayed little interest in social and economic change as these terms have come to be understood since the Mexican, Russian, and anticolonial revolutions. For him, economic improvement and a bridging of class differences were practical requirements of national solidarity and international stature, rather than deeply felt needs of human justice and dignity."[25] Precisely because of its instrumental character, the RPP's doctrine remained vulnerable to rational criticism. Once a secular, republican nation-state seemed securely established, it became legitimate to ask whether Kemalist goals could not be better pursued under a competitive political system. Put differently, the success of Kemalist reforms undermined the long-term legitimacy of the single-party system.[26]

No component of the RPP doctrine provided a permanent justification for an authoritarian single-party system. As Maurice Duverger succinctly states, "The Turkish single-party system was never based upon the doctrine of a single party. It gave no official recognition to the monopoly, made no attempts to justify it by the existence of a classless society or the desire to do away with parliamentary strife and liberal democracy. It was always embarrassed and almost ashamed of the monopoly. The Turkish single party had a bad conscience."[27] Feroz Ahmad agrees:

> The Kemalists denied any affinity with fascism. Unlike the regimes in Rome and Berlin, Ankara accepted liberal principles and the nineteenth century idea of progress. It recognized the rule of law and the importance of the constitutional state. Unlike fascism, there was no denial of the universality of civilization, nor a rejection of rationalism, individualism, and the fundamental equality of man and ethnic groups. The Kemalist regime continued to be transitional in character, preparing the ground for a liberal political and economic system which would replace it in the near future.[28]

Perhaps nothing expresses this transitional nature of authoritarianism and the guilty conscience better than two statements by Atatürk and Inönü. During a discussion of the formation of the Free Republican Party, Atatürk told Fethi Okyar that "our present appearance more or less conforms to that of a dictatorship. Although there is an Assembly, they view us as dictator in the country and abroad. . . . I did not, however, establish the Republic for my own personal benefit. We are all mortals. What will remain behind after I die is an institution of despotism. But I don't want to leave as a legacy to the nation an institution of despotism and to go down in history like this."[29] Inönü expressed the same feeling many years after the transition to democracy: "When I used to see the neighboring countries holding free elections, I used to feel so ashamed that I could not even look at the walls of my room."[30]

In May 1945 Inönü reportedly told Nihat Erim, a rising deputy and a strong supporter of Inönü's initiatives:

> Our present system depends upon the person at the top. This type of government generally makes a brilliant start; they may even go on like this for a while. But there is no end to it. When the person at the helm retires, nobody knows what will be the fate of the regime. Single-party rules have collapsed since they have not transformed themselves into normal democratic forms of government, or at least they have not brought about this transformation at the right time. . . . We should save our country from this fate. We should make a quick transition to serious and established systems of opposition and control. . . . I could spend my lifetime with a single-party regime. But I am concerned about the end. I am concerned about what will happen after my lifetime. We should therefore start the process without delay.[31]

Organizationally, too, the RPP was closer to an old-fashioned cadre party than to a modern totalitarian mass party. Juan J. Linz counts a number of indicators by which one can assess the functional importance of the party in an authoritarian regime: "the number of high officials that were active in the party before entering the elite; the membership figures; the degree of activity indicated by the budget; agit-prop activity; the prestige or power accorded to party officials; the presence of party cells or representatives in other institutions; the importance of training centers; the attention paid to party organs and publications; the vigor of ideological polemics within the party factions."[32] By most of these criteria, the RPP did not appear to be a particularly strong single party. As I pointed out earlier, the RPP engaged in little systematic ideological indoctrination, and the party organization remained inactive most of the time. Perhaps most important for our purposes, the RPP never became a mass mobilizational party; it remained a cadre party, an elite organization dominated by the official bureaucratic elite at the center and local notables in the provinces. The RPP leadership made no notable effort to broaden the party's popular base or to enlist the support of the peasant masses; instead, it concentrated on the small westernized, educated elite.[33] In short, neither doctrinal nor organizational characteristics of the RPP were conducive to or supportive of a permanent authoritarian regime.

The 1945–1950 Turkish transition supports the hypothesis that the nature of the ancien régime has an impact on the type and outcome of a transition.[34] The potentially democratic character of RPP rule made the initiation of the reform process possible, resulting in turn in the transition to democracy with no institutional break with the old regime.

Transitions from Military Rule
(1960–1961, 1971–1973, 1980–1983)

The three transitions from military rule correspond to three military interruptions of the democratic process. Of these, the 1971 intervention was more of a "reequilibration of democracy," since it did not involve suspending the constitution, dissolving the National Assembly, or outlawing political parties.[35] Instead, the military strongly urged the formation of an above party, or technocratic government, behind which it exercised strong political influence. The new government was expected to deal sternly with political violence (with the help of martial law), to bring about constitutional amendments designed to strengthen the executive branch, and to carry out social reforms (especially land reform) provided for by the 1961 constitution. The interim period ended with the normally scheduled parliamentary elections in fall 1973.

As distinct from the 1971 "half coup," the 1960 and 1980 military interventions involved a complete break with existing institutional schemes. In both instances the military wielded significant political influence in the making of new constitutions (see Chapter 3), leading to political regimes rather different from the old ones. In both cases, the military did not intend to establish enduring military regimes but rather to restore democracy within a reasonably short period. More important for our purposes, both military regimes started a reform path to democracy whereby they carefully controlled the conditions and modalities of the transition. In both instances, they extracted important exit guarantees as a price for their extrication from government (see Chapter 5).

There were also important differences between the two. The 1960 intervention was carried out by a group of middle-rank officers who upon assuming power invited a senior general (Cemal Gürsel, commander of the army, who was sent to semiretirement by the DP government) to head the revolutionary committee (the

National Unity Committee [NUC]). In contrast, the 1980 intervention (like that of 1971) was carried out by the top level of the armed forces within the hierarchical chain of command. As a consequence, during the first military regime important differences appeared between the military-as-government (the NUC) and the military-as-institution; there were also conflicts within the NUC. These conflicts occurred between the moderates, who favored the restoration of democracy as soon as possible (in practical terms, this meant a transfer of power to the RPP, since its chief rival, the DP, had been outlawed), and the radicals, who were intent on establishing a long-term military regime ostensibly to carry out radical structural reforms. The conflict ended with the purge of the radicals, opening the way to a relatively quick transition to democracy in fall 1961.

Tensions between the military-as-government and the military-as-institution did not end with the purge, however. In 1961 senior officers with active commands formed an informal umbrella organization called the Armed Forces Union (AFU) to monitor the activities of the NUC. Relations between the two bodies reached a crisis point in June 1961, when the NUC decided to send Air Force commander General Irfan Tansel to Washington as head of the military mission. The AFU ultimatum and the flying of jets over Ankara forced the NUC to rescind its decision and to carry out other changes in the command structure imposed by the AFU.[36] Thus, from that point true power was exercised by the AFU. In contrast, the ruling military council in the period 1980–1983 (the National Security Council) was composed of the five highest-ranking generals in the armed forces, and no conflicts within the NSC or between the NSC and the military-as-institution became a matter of public knowledge.

Another important difference between the two military regimes is found in their attitudes toward civilian political forces. Although the NUC regime (especially its dominant moderate faction) collaborated closely with the main opposition party, the RPP, the NSC regime chose not to collaborate with any political party or any other civilian political institution. Instead, it outlawed all existing political parties and permitted only three of the newly established parties to enter the race for the 1983 parliamentary elections.

Both transitions from military-led governments in 1961 and

1983 are borderline cases between redemocratization initiated by military-as-government and redemocratization led by military-as-institution, as distinguished by Alfred Stepan.[37] In both cases, the military-as-government (the NUC and the NSC) initiated the redemocratization process, but the plan was also supported by the military-as-institution, which thought a long-term military regime would be harmful to its internal unity and cohesion. The Turkish experience also supports the hypothesis that a military-led transition is likely to leave "institutional traces" such as autonomy and tutelary powers for the military-as-institution.[38]

Perhaps an even more important difference between the two military regimes is seen in the nature of the policies they followed. The 1960 coup resembled moderating coups in that its main objective was to resolve a constitutional crisis rather than to make radical changes in the social and political structure. NUC legislative activities remained essentially limited to making a new constitution, a new electoral law, and a few other laws. The NSC regime, on the other hand, passed more than six hundred laws affecting almost all aspects of social, economic, and political structures—including laws regarding political parties, trade unions, voluntary associations, public professional organizations, universities, radio and television, local governments, the judiciary, and emergency regimes. Except for its relatively short duration, in some respects the NSC regime is reminiscent of the bureaucratic-authoritarian military regimes in Latin America and elsewhere.

Guillermo O'Donnell and others have argued that the emergence of bureaucratic-authoritarian regimes (BA) as a new type of authoritarian rule in Latin America has been linked to the failure of import substitution–based industrialization (ISI).[39] The early phases of this industrialization strategy gave rise to populist coalitions that brought together national industrialists and the emerging urban working class. Both components of the populist coalition benefited from this expansionist policy: import substituting industrialists were given various investment inducements and were heavily protected against foreign competition by import quotas, tariffs, and foreign exchange regulations; the urban working class, in turn, obtained employment opportunities, union rights, welfare benefits, and relatively higher wages because the growth of the domestic market was supposed to further stimulate the ISI.

The early, easy phase of the ISI, however, was soon exhausted. Once the limits of growth of domestic markets had been reached, the inefficient, internationally noncompetitive national industries failed to produce the necessary foreign exchange earnings. Thus, ISI-based economies faced severe problems such as balance-of-payment deficits, foreign exchange shortages, low or negative growth rates, inflation, and unemployment. The economic crisis, in turn, led to the radicalization of the popular sector (the industrial working class) and to increased political polarization. The resultant military-led BA regimes attempted to solve the problem by moving the economic structure in a more free-market, export-oriented direction and demobilizing the activated popular sector by restricting its political participation opportunities.

In Turkey the NSC regime, like its Latin American counterparts, followed a period of deep economic crisis marked by high rates of inflation, a shortage of intermediary and consumer goods, and a severe foreign exchange shortage brought about by the failure of ISI policies. As in Latin America, this crisis marked the end of the populist coalition forged by the DP and the Justice Party (JP), the radicalization of the urban working class, and the growth of authoritarian tendencies within the middle class because of a fear of communism. Like its Latin American counterparts, the resultant NSC regime pursued policies aimed at shifting the basis of the economy from an import substitution to an export promotion model while restricting the mobilization of the popular sector. Indeed, an analysis of the 1982 constitution and other laws during the NSC period clearly suggests that one fundamental aim of the NSC regime was to demobilize the working class and depoliticize the society at large, especially by outlawing all cooperation between political parties and other civil society institutions such as trade unions, professional organizations, and voluntary associations. In short, just as the Latin American BAs differed from the earlier moderating coups, the NSC regime differed from the 1960 intervention in its longer duration and especially in its aim to fundamentally restructure the economy and society.

The basis of the NSC economic policies had been laid by the deposed minority government of Süleyman Demirel in what came to be known as the January 24 measures. As Henri Barkey explains, "On January 24, 1980, the Demirel government announced what would turn out to be the most significant set of measures since 1960. Intent on revitalizing the economy with a new program, the government abandoned the inward-oriented, import substitution guided political economy in favor of an export-driven one." Barkey argues, however, that the liberalization policies initiated in January 1980 could not have survived without the coup. In the first place, the military intervention "boosted, and even rescued, the January 24, 1980, measures. Second, it paved the way for the restructuring of the state's political foundations, without which the long-term economic transformation would not have materialized."[40] The NSC regime kept the architect of the January 24 measures, Turgut Özal, in place; it even promoted him from chair of the State Planning Organization to deputy prime minister in charge of economic affairs. When he became prime minister as head of his newly formed Motherland Party in November 1983, Özal continued and expanded these policies, which by now seem to have reached a point of no return.

One similarity between the 1960 and 1980 interventions is that in both cases, especially in the case of the 1960 intervention, the political influence of the outgoing military regime continued long after the transition elections. The military leaders, concerned about the increasing popularity of the JP—which appeared to be a direct heir to the DP—forced the party leaders to agree on the propaganda to be used for the approaching 15 October 1961 elections: "On 31 August the party leaders began their round-table conference under military auspices and issued on 5 September a joint declaration in which they promised: (1) not to question or exploit for political purposes the Revolution of 27 May; (2) to protect Atatürk's reforms; (3) not to exploit Islam for political ends; (4) not to exploit the verdicts of the Yassıada trials."[41] The practice of forcing party leaders to agree on certain principles deemed necessary by the military continued after the transition. On 24 October 1961 the party leaders, at the prodding of the military commanders, signed a protocol whereby they agreed not to reinstate "officers retired by the NUC and not to seek an amnesty for the Democrats sentenced at Yassıada. They also promised to have General Gürsel elected President of the Republic, and to accept Inönü as Prime Minister."[42] This was the price party leaders had to pay for military consent for convening the newly elected parliament.

Threats of a new military intervention continued until the suppression of the coup attempt by Talat Aydemir, commander of the War College, on 22 February 1962. In the aftermath of the 1983 transition, in contrast, there were no such instances of open arm-twisting or coup threats by the military, simply because there was no need for them. The leader of the NSC regime had already been elected president of the republic for a seven-year period; other NSC members enjoyed the privileges and immunities that came with their membership in the newly created Presidential Council; and other exit guarantees for the military, incorporated in the 1982 constitution, were firmly in place (see Chapter 5).

The Crises and Breakdowns of Democratic Rule: 1960, 1971, 1980

The three military interventions in recent Turkish politics resulted from profound crises in democratic rule. In general, two approaches have been used to explain democratic breakdowns across the world. One tends "to emphasize the structural charac-teristics of societies—socioeconomic infrastructures that act as a constraining condition, limiting the choice of political actors. Some scholars focus on the underlying social conflicts, particular-ly class conflicts, that in their view make the stability of liberal democratic institutions unlikely, if not impossible." The other approach, followed most notably by Juan Linz and Alfred Stepan in their classic work on the breakdown of democratic regimes, starts from the assumption that social and political actors "have certain choices that can increase or decrease the probability of the persistence and stability of a regime." Although the authors do not ignore basic social, economic, and cultural variables, they focus on "more strictly political variables" in the belief that "polit-ical processes actually precipitate the ultimate breakdown." Thus, they advance the hypothesis that "the democratic regimes under study had at one point or another a reasonable chance to survive and become fully consolidated, but that certain characteristics and actions of relevant actors—institutions as well as individu-als—decreased the probability of such a development."[43] The three breakdowns in Turkey provide ample support for this hypothesis.

The 1960 breakdown.   Turkey's first extensive experience with democracy (1946–1960) ended with the military intervention on 27 May 1960. During this period, two main parties (the DP and the RPP) competed for power, and the DP won the 1950, 1954, and 1957 elections with substantial margins. The ideological distance between the two parties was not great; they differed mostly in their attitudes toward the proper role of the state, bureaucracy, private enterprise, and local initiative, as well as toward peasant participation in politics. Whereas the RPP-oriented national elite had a more tutelary conception of development, the provincial elites within the DP emphasized local initiative and immediate satisfaction of local expectations.[44] Still, as Feroz Ahmad, an acute observer of Turkish politics, has argued with regard to the 1950 elections, "there was hardly any difference between the pro-grammes of the two parties. The RPP was willing to remove the six principles from the constitution if it was re-elected and it bent over backwards to appease the private sector and the clericalists in order to compete with the Democrats and the National Party. . . . They differed about as much as the Republican and Democratic parties in the United States and had more in common than the Labour and Conservative parties in Britain."[45]

Despite the nonideological nature of the partisan conflict, relations between the two major parties quickly deteriorated. Especially after the 1957 elections, the DP reacted to its declining support by resorting to increasingly authoritarian measures against the opposition, which only made the opposition more uncompromising and vociferous. These measures included, among others, tightening the press law, jailing scores of journalists, demoting the province of Kırsehir for voting for the opposition Republican Nation Party in the 1954 elections, using the state radio in a one-sided manner, banning political meetings and demonstrations except during election campaigns, barring judicial review of acts forcing civil servants to take early retirement, forbidding opposition parties to mount mixed lists at elections, and changing the standing orders of the Assembly to stifle opposition criticisms. Celal Bayar, president of the republic, described and defended these measures as "putting an end to refined democracy."[46]

The last straw in this long chain of authoritarian measures came in April 1960, when the government party established a parliamentary committee of inquiry to investigate "subversive" activities of the RPP and some of the press. The committee was given extraordinary judicial and administrative powers. Many opposition members were now convinced that a point of no return had been reached and that the channels of democratic change had become clogged. The ensuing public unrest, student demonstrations in Istanbul and Ankara, and clashes between students and police led to a declaration of martial law, which put the armed forces in the unwanted position of suppressing the opposition on behalf of a government for whose policies they had little sympathy. The military intervened on 27 May 1960, with the support of the opposition.

What or who is to be blamed for the failure of this first extended Turkish experiment with democratic politics? One reason involved the nature of the DP, which was a coalition of diverse anti-RPP forces. The DP leadership was convinced that the party "could retain its unity only by keeping its ranks mobilized against the RPP. This was realized partly by accusing the RPP of subverting the government through its hold on the bureaucracy, and partly by raising the specter of a return of the RPP to power."[47] Second, the DP leaders—having been socialized into politics under RPP rule—had inherited many attitudes, norms, and orientations that were more in harmony with single-party rule than with a competitive party system, including a belief that a popular mandate entitled the government party to unrestricted use of political power. Combined with the Ottoman-Turkish cultural legacy, which barely distinguished between political opposition and treasonable activity, this attitude left little room for a legitimate opposition.[48]

Another factor that eventually led to the breakdown of the democratic regime was the conflict between the DP and the public bureaucracy. The bureaucracy, the main pillar of the single-party regime, retained its RPP loyalties under multiparty politics and resisted the DP's efforts to consolidate its political power. In the eyes of DP leaders, this amounted to an unwarranted obstruction of the "national will." The bureaucrats, however, saw it as their duty to protect the public interest against efforts to use state funds for political patronage purposes. They were also deeply troubled by the DP government's careless attitude toward the rule of law and by its relatively permissive policies toward religious activities, which the bureaucrats considered a betrayal of the Kemalist legacy of secularism. These negative attitudes were shared by civilian officials and military officers.

Finally, all bureaucratic groups (both civilian and military) experienced a loss of social status and political influence under the DP regime and were also adversely affected in terms of relative income. The DP's economic policies consisted of rapid import substitution–based industrialization and the modernization of agriculture, largely through external borrowing and inflationary financing. Although a relatively high rate of economic growth was achieved in the 1950s, income distribution became much more inequitable, with salaried groups hit particularly hard by the inflationary policies. The 1960 coup therefore was quickly accepted by military officers and civilian officials for economic as well as other reasons.

This analysis implies that the 1960 military intervention was not inevitable. The string of antidemocratic measures described here, culminating in the establishment of the notorious inquiry committee, left no doubt in many people's minds—including the RPP leaders and many military officers—that the DP government could not be expected to submit itself to free and honest elections. Most observers agree that a government call for early elections would have saved the situation even in spring 1960.[49] Indeed, at that time Menderes seems to have vacillated between making such an announcement and tightening the antidemocratic measures, and it is widely believed it was Bayar who pushed him toward the latter option.[50]

Thus, the disloyalty of the DP government toward the democratic regime increasingly led the RPP to act as a disloyal opponent of the government.[51] This does not mean the RPP actually "knocked on the barracks" for armed forces support or had advance knowledge of the intervention. A day after the coup General Gürsel, the leader of the coup, reportedly called İnönü, the leader of the RPP, to tell him "we are at fault with you, my general. We did not inform you in advance of our action. But we knew that had we done so, you would have wanted us to give up. We had nothing else to do. We beg for your forgiveness."[52] For his part, İnönü gave the coup the green light with such statements as "from now on even I cannot save you" and "they [the DP leaders] think that the Turkish nation is not as dignified as the Korean nation" (a clear reference to the recent overthrow of the Syngman Rhee dictatorship in South Korea). Metin Toker concludes that if İnönü had been forced to make a choice between a DP dictatorship and a military revolution at that time, he would have opted for the latter.[53]

The 1971 crisis: Coup by memorandum. Although the JP won an absolute majority of National Assembly seats in the 1965 and 1969 elections, toward the end of the 1960s the JP government, led by Süleyman Demirel, became increasingly unable to cope with the worsening political situation. In part as a result of the more liberal atmosphere under the 1961 constitution, extreme left- and right-wing groups appeared on the political scene. This development was followed by increased acts of violence such as murders, kidnappings, bombings, and bank robberies—especially by extremist youth groups. Student radicalism was accompanied by increased radicalization of the working class, culminating in a bloody workers' uprising in Istanbul and Kocaeli on 15–16 March 1970. Landless peasants began to occupy private farms.

The crisis was aggravated by the activities of various conspiratorial groups within the military. These radical officers, frustrated by the successive electoral victories of the conservative JP, aimed to establish a long-term military regime, ostensibly to carry out radical social reforms. In fact, the military memorandum of 12 March 1971 that forced the JP government to resign was a last-minute move by top military commanders to forestall a radical coup. Once the high command of the armed forces established control, it quickly forced the leading radical officers to retire— including five generals, one admiral, and thirty-five colonels on 17 March. [54]

The so-called 12 March regime did not go as far as dissolving the parliament and assuming power directly. It was a coup by memorandum signed by the chief of the general staff and the three force commanders. The memorandum read as follows:

> 1. The Parliament and the Government, through their sustained policies, views and actions, have driven our country into anarchy, fratricidal strife, and social and economic unrest. They have caused the public to lose all hope of rising to the level of contemporary civilization which was set for us by Atatürk as a goal, and have failed to realize the reforms stipulated by the

Constitution. The future of the Turkish Republic is therefore
seriously threatened.

2. The assessment by the Parliament, in a spirit above partisan considerations, of the solutions needed to eliminate the concern and disillusionment of the Turkish Armed Forces, which
have sprung from the bosom of the Turkish nation, over this
grave situation; and the formation, within the context of democratic principles, of a strong and credible government, which
will neutralize the current anarchical situation and which,
inspired by Atatürk's views, will implement the reformist laws
envisaged by the Constitution, are considered essential.

3. Unless this is done quickly, the Turkish Armed Forces are
determined to take over the administration of the State in accordance with the powers vested in them by the laws to protect and
preserve the Turkish Republic.

Please be informed.[55]

As was demanded in the second paragraph of the memorandum, the resignation of the Demirel government was followed by
the formation of an above-party, or technocratic, government led
by veteran RPP politician Nihat Erim, who resigned from his
party to become a more suitable candidate for the premiership of
this new government. The Erim government included five ministers from the JP, three from the RPP, and one from the Reliance
Party, as well as fourteen technocrats from outside the
parliament;[56] it duly received a vote of confidence from the
National Assembly. The new government was expected to deal
sternly with political violence (with the help of martial law), to
develop constitutional amendments designed to strengthen the
executive, and to carry out the social reforms (particularly land
reform) provided for by the 1961 constitution. The interim government accomplished its first two objectives. Political violence
was effectively stamped out. The constitution was revised exten-
sively in 1971 and 1973, with a view to not only strengthen executive authority but also to limit certain civil liberties seen as
responsible for the emergence of political extremism and violence.
Ironically, the constitutional amendments proposed by the military and adopted by parliament were very much in line with—
indeed far more thorough than—the ones advocated by the JP,
which felt the liberal 1961 constitution was a "luxury" that made
governance of the country impossible.[57] The interim regime
failed, however, in its third objective to carry out social reforms,
not only because of the conservative majority in parliament but

also because of the purge of radical officers following the 12 March memorandum.

The 1971 military intervention, which ended with parliamentary elections in fall 1973, can be characterized as a half coup in which the military chose to govern from behind the scenes instead of taking over directly. If the intervention occurred in part because of the failure of the JP government to cope with political terrorism, a more deep-seated cause was the distrust many military officers felt toward the JP. Thus, in a sense the 1971 intervention still reflected the old cleavage between the centralist bureaucratic elite and the periphery forces that continued to command an electoral majority. In both its political consequences and the general direction of its policies, this intervention stood as a "way station" between the 1960 and 1980 interventions.

The 1980 breakdown.   The immediate reason for the 1980 military intervention was the growing political violence and terrorism that between 1975 and 1980 left more than five thousand people dead and three times as many wounded (the equivalent of Turkish losses in the War of Independence). Acts of violence—which became particularly acute between 1978 and 1980—also included armed assaults, acts of sabotage, kidnappings, bank robberies, occupation and destruction of workplaces, and bombings. Forty-nine radical leftist groups were involved in left-wing terrorism, whereas right-wing terrorism was concentrated in the "idealist" organizations with unofficial links to the Nationalist Action Party (NAP).

Thus, in a sense the pattern that had led to the 1971 military intervention was repeated, only on a much larger and more alarming scale. As in the early 1970s, governments in the late 1970s were unable to cope with the problem, even though martial law was in effect in much of the country. Under the Turkish constitutional system, martial law entails the transfer of police functions to military authorities, the restriction or suspension of civil liberties, and the creation of military martial law courts to try offenses associated with the causes that led to the declaration of martial law. Thus, the procedure is constitutional, albeit highly authoritarian and restrictive. During the crisis of the late 1970s, however, even martial law could not contain the violence, in part because of the infiltration of the police forces by right-wing and left-wing extremists and in part because of the general erosion of state authority as a result of growing political polarization in the country, as is discussed later. A harmful side effect of martial law is the seemingly inevitable politicization of the armed forces, or the militarization of political conflict, which may pave the way for full-scale military intervention. Indeed, all three military interventions in recent Turkish history were preceded by martial law regimes instituted by civilian governments.

At a deeper level, the incidence of political violence reflected a growing ideological polarization in Turkey between the NAP and, to a much lesser extent, the National Salvation Party (NSP) on the right and many small radical groups on the left. The NSP was not involved in violence, but its Islamic themes helped to undermine the regime's legitimacy among those committed to the Kemalist legacy of secularism, including the military. The balance of political forces in parliament and the inability or unwillingness of the two major parties (the RPP and the JP) to agree on a grand coalition or a minority government arrangement gave the two minor parties enormous bargaining—more correctly, blackmailing—power, which they used to obtain important ministries and to colonize them with their own partisans. This fact seems crucial in explaining the crisis of the system. As the experience of many countries has shown, antisystem parties can perhaps be tolerated in opposition, but their entry into the government tends to place too heavy a load on the system to be handled by democratic means.

The radical left, unlike the radical right, was not represented in the parliament, but extreme leftist ideologies had many supporters among students, teachers, and some sectors of the industrial working class. Political polarization also affected and undermined the public bureaucracy. At no time in recent Turkish history had public agencies been as divided and politicized as they were in the late 1970s. Changes of government were followed by extensive purges in all ministries, involving not only the top personnel but also many middle- and lower-ranking civil servants. Partisanship became a norm in the civil service, which until the mid-1970s had retained an essentially nonpolitical character.

A related phenomenon that contributed to decreased legitimacy of the political system was the *immobilisme* of the government and parliament during much of the 1970s. The narrow majorities in the parliament and the heterogeneous nature of the governing coalitions (whether the Nationalist Front government or the Ecevit government) meant new policies could be initiated only with great difficulty. In the context of pressing economic troubles (such as high inflation, major deficits in the international trade balance, shortages of investment and consumer goods, and unemployment) and international problems (such as the Cyprus crisis and the U.S. arms embargo), governmental inability to take courageous policy decisions aggravated the legitimacy crisis. Put differently, the lack of efficacy and effectiveness delegitimated the regime. Perhaps the most telling example of governmental failure of performance was the inability of the Turkish Grand National Assembly to elect a president of the republic in 1980; the six-month-old deadlock ended only with the military coup of 12 September. Other examples of deadlocks abounded, particularly in matters of economic and foreign policy.

The political dynamics that led to the 1980 intervention support observations made by Juan J. Linz to explain the breakdown of democratic regimes. Linz has argued that "an indicator of semi-loyal behavior, and a source of perceptions leading to questions about the loyalty of a party to the system, is a willingness to encourage, tolerate, cover up, treat leniently, excuse or justify the actions of other participants that go beyond the limits of peaceful, legitimate patterns of politics in a democracy." Parties may "reject the means as undignified and extreme, but excuse them and . . . not denounce them publicly because of agreement with the goals so pursued. Such agreement in principle and disagreement on tactics is a frequent indicator of semiloyalty. . . . Unequal application of justice to the illegal acts of different disloyal oppositions contributes decisively to the image of semiloyalty."[58]

Indeed, a characteristic feature of the years leading to the 1980 breakdown was the widespread perception that when they headed the government the major democratic parties (the JP and the RPP) did not apply justice equally to terrorists of the right and the left. The JP frequently accused the RPP-based Ecevit government (1978–1979) for being lenient toward communists and Kurdish separatists. Thus, JP leader Demirel, in two letters to President Fahri Korutürk (on 21 February 1979 and in August 1979), charged that the Ecevit government had not implemented the laws against communist and separatist terrorists and had protected "gangs that committed murders."[59] Demirel also stated that leftists (meaning RPP supporters) could not be nationalists and that the Ecevit government was based on leftist centers of agitation.[60] Similarly, Faruk Sükan, a Democratic Party deputy who served as one of three deputy prime ministers in the Ecevit government, stated in a letter written to President Korutürk on 11 September 1979, just before his resignation, that the government had calculated to preserve the balance within the RPP and the National Assembly and had thus made concessions to separatists; therefore, it had become impossible to fight anarchy and separatism.[61] Ecevit vehemently denied the charges that his government was lenient toward separatists and anarchists.[62]

Ecevit and other RPP spokespersons leveled similar charges against the JP-dominated Nationalist Front governments (1975–1977 and 1977) for having protected right-wing terrorists. Many believed right-wing terror was connected with the Nationalist Action Party, and the NAP's presence as a partner in the Nationalist Front coalitions made these charges more credible than the countercharges of Demirel and the JP. Thus, Ecevit frequently stated that the NAP-connected right-wing terrorists were nurtured and protected by the Nationalist Front governments.[63] An RPP no-confidence motion against Demirel's minority government on 24 June 1980 stated that "individual or organized terror was transformed into a widespread mass terror by the bullies who benefited from the protection of government and made the government their captive."[64] In the months following the formation of Demirel's minority government, Ecevit made statements such as

> bandits imitating the SS and the Gestapo are perpetrating massacres against groups of innocent people; real or pseudo government forces are perpetrating torture[s] against the people to an extent far greater than those committed by the Gestapo leaders in countries under their occupation. (15 February 1980)

> in recent years the nurturing of the right-wing militants under semi-official protection provoked the extreme-left terrorism. The present government is not evenhanded toward these groups. (20 April 1980)

> the government is in the arms of the NAP and fascism. Turkey is nearly under the occupation of a fascist or Nazi force. (21 May 1980)

> today the government is headed by a person maddened by the
> desire to bring fascism to the country as soon as possible. (12
> July 1980)[65]

> political murderers are getting support from the government.
> Demirel is not only the head of government but the head of ban-
> dits because he protects them.[66]

Predictably, Demirel has always denied the charge of being
lenient toward or protective of right-wing terrorists, saying
"nobody can make me say that rightists and nationalists are com-
mitting murders."[67] Privately, however, he reportedly admitted to
a journalist that a "murder network" probably existed within the
NAP: "they are cruel and merciless. If I can get hold of them, I
will uproot them."[68]

The charges and countercharges of being lenient toward fascist, communist, or separatist terror reflected the growing polarization in the second half of the 1970s. Just as the JP was pulled to
the right by its partnership with the NAP and the NSP, the RPP
was pulled to the left by the small but vocal radical groups to its
left. Thus, the party system displayed some of the functional characteristics of an extreme (or polarized) multiparty system (especially the centrifugal drive associated with such a system), even
though its format remained closer to a moderate multiparty
model with an essentially four-party structure produced by the
1977 elections.[69] Still, the ideological differences between the two
major parties were not great enough to preclude a grand coalition
of the two. An accommodation between them would have been
welcomed by most of the important political groups in Turkey,
including the business community, the leading trade union confederation (Türk-Is), the military, the press, and the president of
the republic, and it would have been acceptable to a majority of
the JP and RPP deputies. A government based on the joint support of the two parties would probably have been strong enough
to deal effectively and evenhandedly with political violence, to
stop political polarization, and to restore a degree of impartiality
to the public bureaucracy.

Several opportunities for such a coalition were missed.
Demirel always remained cool to the idea, and Ecevit sought the
JP's cooperation only when he was unable to form a government.
Immediately after the 1977 elections, when the RPP emerged as
the largest party—only slightly short of a majority in the National

Assembly—Ecevit ruled out a coalition with either the JP or the NAP, arguing that the two parties shared the same conception of democracy. Demirel, in turn, refused to support Ecevit's minority government.[70] When his government failed to receive a vote of confidence, Ecevit offered Demirel three alternatives: an RPP-JP coalition headed by the RPP leader, by the JP leader, or by an independent.[71] Although some JP deputies supported the offer, Demirel rejected it as "against the nature of things."[72] Years after the 1980 intervention, Demirel still defended his attitude, saying "one can be united and together only in truth. One cannot be united and together in error. There is only one correct solution for each problem. . . . If the correct solution has been proposed and it has turned out to be impossible to agree on it, it is unfair and unjust to jointly blame both the one who made the proposal and the one who did not accept it."[73]

When Ecevit formed his government in early 1978 with the support of twelve defectors from the JP, he did not seek the JP's cooperation. During Ecevit's premiership, the JP seems to have considered a future JP-RPP coalition only on the condition of early elections, a condition the RPP was sure to reject.[74]

A final missed opportunity came when the Ecevit government resigned in October 1979, following the by-elections on 14 October in which the JP emerged as the clear victor and the RPP share of the vote fell considerably—from 41.4 percent in 1977 to 29.1 percent. At that point, Ecevit offered to support a JP minority government to enable it to remain in power without outside NAP support.[75] But Demirel preferred to form his minority government with the outside support of the NSP and the NAP. During the rule of the JP minority government, Ecevit repeated his offer several times for either a JP-RPP government or a so-called reparation government (*onarım hükûmeti*), to be joined by the NSP as well.[76] Demirel remained indifferent to these proposals, as well as to any meaningful dialogue with the RPP on measures to be taken to combat terrorism. He reportedly told a journalist that to hear the word "dialogue . . . made him nauseate[d]."[77]

In hindsight, one can only speculate whether an RPP-JP coalition might have prevented the breakdown. In interviews in the mid-1980s, Ecevit repeated his view that the military intervention could have been avoided if an RPP-JP government had been formed and a president of the republic been elected.[78] Demirel believes, however, that by their very nature certain problems are not susceptible to compromise and that it is a mistake to blame political leaders for not having reached a compromise on such matters. The real causes of the intervention should not be confused with the apparent causes. If the military intended "to abolish the constitution and to make a new one, to take over the government, to occupy positions of power, and to purge certain [political] cadres," those moves could not have been avoided by a collaboration between the two parties.[79]

Statements by military leaders both before and after the 1980 intervention, however, make it clear that they had considered an RPP-JP government highly desirable and saw the lack of such cooperation as the primary cause of the breakdown. On 6 September 1979, for example, Admiral Bülent Ulusu, commander of the navy (who later became prime minister under the NSC regime), privately told a journalist that the only way to save the country was for "the two parties to get together and form a government"; otherwise, a military intervention would be inevitable.[80] Also, the memorandum to the president of the republic from the chief of the general staff and four force commanders on 27 December 1979 stated that it was the duty of the government, as well as of other political parties, to save the country from the anarchy, terrorism, and secessionism that were escalating rapidly. The letter invited all political parties to "unite in the direction of the principles of the Constitution and Kemalism" and to "jointly take all the [necessary] measures against such actions as anarchy, terrorism and secessionism that aim at the destruction of the state."[81] According to some reports, however, in the aftermath of the by-elections on 14 October 1979, the military was no longer interested in a JP-RPP coalition because a decision to intervene had already been made.[82]

Nevertheless, it would be erroneous to attribute the lack of cooperation between the two major parties chiefly to the uncompromising attitude of, and deep personal animosity between, their leaders. The logic of the prevailing political situation also dictated polarization. On the right, the rising star of Ecevit and the RPP created a deep concern because Demirel and other Nationalist Front leaders identified the RPP with the extreme left, if not with communism. Demirel expressed the belief that the RPP was "an enemy of the regime" and that it did not hide "its passion

for socialism and collectivism." The RPP's penchant for cooperatives would lead to an "Eastern type cooperativism."[83] Similar
fears existed on the left. The RPP and other leftists believed the JP,
in cooperation with the NAP, was intent on bringing fascism to
Turkey.

Whether such statements by both sides accurately reflected
their perceptions or were simply devices to frighten and mobilize
their own followings is difficult to tell.[84] Both factors likely played
a role, but even if the latter strategy were the case, it worked. By
mobilizing fears of communism, the JP was able to lead the
Nationalist Front government and to increase its share of the vote
from 29.8 percent in 1973 to 36.9 percent in 1977 to roughly 45.0
percent in the by-elections in 1979. Similarly, the fear of fascism
was an important cause of the significant increase in the share of
the RPP vote between 1973 and 1977, which rose from 33.3 percent to 41.4 percent. Because the probability of coming to power
alone was strong for both parties, from a purely electoral point of
view it made sense to further polarize the situation rather than
share the responsibilities of power. Further, there has been an
unchanging tendency in Turkish politics to see the struggle for
power as a zero-sum game, as was alluded to earlier.

A crisis of democracy often involves "knocking at the barracks" to seek out army support, even by members of loyal,
regime-supporting parties.[85] In the years leading to the 1980
breakdown, we see many examples of such behavior. For example, the NAP, whose loyalty to the democratic regime was dubious at best, often insisted on the proclamation of martial law, hop-
ing it would be able to manipulate martial law in its own interests
with the help of sympathizers within the army.[86] The party's central executive committee's statement on 1–2 October 1978 was
widely considered an open incitement to a military takeover.[87]
Some politicians—even ministers—from such regime-supporting
parties as the JP, the RPP, and the Republican Reliance Party have
reportedly complained to military commanders about the behavior of their own leaders, thus contributing to an atmosphere supportive of a military intervention.[88]

The events leading to the 1980 intervention support the observation that a coup is unlikely to happen unless it has the support
of some important civilian groups. Many believe the military

deliberately delayed action, assuming that the continuation and aggravation of the crisis would further support the intervention.[89]

* * *

To summarize, none of the three breakdowns of democracy in Turkey seem to be the inevitable outcome of deep-seated structural or sociological causes. In all cases the behavior of the leaders of political parties looms large as a factor leading to the breakdown. The power vacuum into which the military moved in 1971 and 1980 was created by the actions of disloyal oppositions on both the left and the right and by the semiloyal behavior of the major democratic parties.

NOTES

1. On the waves of democratization, see Samuel P. Huntington, *The Third Wave: Democratization in the Late Twentieth Century* (Norman: University of Oklahoma Press, 1991), 13–26.

2. The 1971 intervention is not counted here since it did not involve the dissolution of parliament and a complete suspension of political party activities, although this interim period is discussed later.

3. Quoted in Metin Toker, *Demokrasimizin Ismet Pasa'lı Yılları: Tek Partiden Çok Partiye, 1944–1950* (From Single Party to Multiparty: Our Years of Democracy with Ismet Pasha, 1944–1950) (Ankara: Bilgi Yayınevi, 1990), 37–38.

4. Quoted in Kemal Karpat, *Turkey's Politics: The Transition to a Multi-Party System* (Princeton: Princeton University Press, 1959), 141.

5. Quoted in Toker, *Tek Partiden Çok Partiye*, 75–76.

6. Ibid., 80–81, 90–91.

7. Karpat, *Turkey's Politics*, 148–149.

8. Ibid., 154–155; Mahmut Gologlu, *Demokrasiye Geçis: 1946–1950* (Transition to Democracy) (Istanbul: Kaynak Yayınları, 1982), 46–52.

9. Gologlu, *Demokrasiye Geçis*, 65; *Cumhuriyet* and *Vatan* (Istanbul dailies), 25 July 1946.

10. Quoted in Karpat, *Turkey's Politics*, 191–192.

11. Gologlu, *Demokrasiye Geçis*, 190.

12. On the reform mode of democratic transitions, see Huntington, *The Third Wave*, 124–142; Scott Mainwaring and Donald Share, "Transitions Through Transaction: Democratization in Brazil and Spain," in W. A. Selcher, ed., *Political Liberalization in Brazil: Dynamics, Dilemmas, and Future Prospects* (Boulder: Westview Press, 1986), 177–179; Alfred Stepan, "Paths Toward Redemocratization: Theoretical and Comparative Considerations," in Guillermo O'Donnell, Philippe C. Schmitter, and Laurence Whitehead, eds., *Transitions from Authoritarian Rule:*

Comparative Perspectives (Baltimore: Johns Hopkins University Press, 1986), 72–78.

13. Huntington, *The Third Wave*, 123–124. Adam Przeworski argues in the same vein that extrication can result only from an understanding between reformers in the goverment and moderates in the opposition: "Extrication is possible if (1) an agreement can be reached between Reformers and Moderates to establish institutions under which the social forces they represent would have a significant political presence in the democratic system, (2) Reformers can deliver the consent of Hardliners or neutralize them, and (3) Moderates can control Radicals." *Democracy and the Market: Political and Economic Reforms in Eastern Europe and Latin America* (Cambridge: Cambridge University Press, 1991), 68.

14. Toker, *Tek Partiden Çok Partiye*, 210–234; Feroz Ahmad, *The Turkish Experiment with Democracy, 1950–1975* (Boulder: Westview Press, 1977), 26–27.

15. Quoted in Toker, *Tek Partiden Çok Partiye*, 40–41.

16. Przeworski, *Democracy and the Market*, 68–70.

17. Huntington, *The Third Wave*, 174–192.

18. Karpat, *Turkey's Politics*, 140–143; Çetin Yetkin, *Türkiye'de Tek Parti Yönetimi, 1930–1945* (Single-Party Rule in Turkey, 1930–1945) (Istanbul: Altın Kitaplar Yayınevi, 1983), 225–254; Rıfkı Salim Burçak, *Türkiye'de Demokrasiye Geçis* (Transition to Democracy in Turkey) (Istanbul: Olgaç Matbaası, 1979), 38–56; Hakan Yılmaz, "Democratization from Above in Response to the International Context: Turkey, 1945–1950," *New Perspectives on Turkey* 17 (fall 1997): 1–37.

19. Bernard Lewis, *The Emergence of Modern Turkey* (London: Oxford University Press, 1968), 313–315.

20. Ahmad, *The Turkish Experiment*, 24.

21. Ilkay Sunar, *State and Society in the Politics of Turkey's Development* (Ankara: A. Ü. Siyasal Bilgiler Fakültesi Yayını, 1974), 80–81; see also Ahmet N. Yücekök, *Siyaset Sosyolojisi Açısından Türkiye'de Parlamentonun Evrimi* (The Evolution of Parliament in Turkey) (Ankara: A. Ü. Siyasal Bilgiler Fakültesi Yayını, 1983), 120–121; Lewis, *The Emergence of Modern Turkey*, 317.

22. Cem Erogul, *Demokrat Parti: Tarihi ve Ideolojisi* (Democratic Party: Its History and Ideology) (Ankara: A. Ü. Siyasal Bilgiler Fakültesi Yayını, 1970), 58.

23. On the distinction between mentalities and ideologies, see Juan J. Linz, "Totalitarian and Authoritarian Regimes," in Fred I. Greenstein and Nelson W. Polsby, eds., *Handbook of Political Science, Vol. 3: Macropolitical Theory* (Reading, Mass.: Addison-Wesley, 1975), 257–259; on the RPP's positivist mentality, see Taner Timur, *Türk Devrimi: Tarihi Anlamı ve Felsefi Temeli* (Turkish Revolution: Its Historical Meaning and Philosophical Foundation) (Ankara: A. Ü. Siyasal Bilgiler Fakültesi Yayını, 1968), 112–116; Serif Mardin, "Religion and Secularism in Turkey," in Ali Kazancıgil and Ergun Özbudun, eds., *Atatürk: Founder of a Modern State* (London: C. Hurst, 1981), 191–219.

24. *Atatürk'ün Söylev ve Demeçleri* (Atatürk's Speeches), Vol. 2 (Ankara: Türk Inkılap Tarihi Enstitüsü Yayınları, 1959), 275.

25. Dankwart A. Rustow, "Atatürk as Founder of a State," in *Prof. Dr. Yavuz Abadan'a Armagan* (Ankara: A. Ü. Siyasal Bilgiler Fakültesi Yayını, 1969), 569.

26. On the distinction between instrumental and expressive ideologies as a source of legitimacy for single-party regimes, see Clement H. Moore, "The Single Party as Source of Legitimacy," in Samuel P. Huntington and Clement H. Moore, eds., *Authoritarian Politics in Modern Society: The Dynamics of Established One-Party Systems* (New York: Basic Books, 1970), 48–72.

27. Maurice Duverger, *Political Parties: Their Organization and Activity in the Modern State* (New York: Wiley, 1959), 277.

28. Feroz Ahmad, "The Political Economy of Kemalism," in Ali Kazancıgil and Ergun Özbudun, eds., *Atatürk: Founder of a Modern State* (London: C. Hurst, 1981), 159.

29. Fethi Okyar, *Üç Devirde Bir Adam* (A Man in Three Periods) (Istanbul: Tercüman Yayınları, 1980), 392–393.

30. Quoted in Toker, *Tek Partiden Çok Partiye,* 17.

31. Ibid., 57.

32. Juan J. Linz, "An Authoritarian Regime: Spain," in Erik Allardt and Stein Rokkan, eds., *Mass Politics: Studies in Political Sociology* (New York: Free Press, 1970), 264.

33. Frederick W. Frey, *The Turkish Political Elite* (Cambridge: MIT Press, 1965), 40–43.

34. Linz and Stepan argue that "the characteristics of the previous nondemocratic regime have profound implications for the transition *paths* available and the *tasks* different countries face when they begin their struggles to develop consolidated democracies." Juan J. Linz and Alfred Stepan, *Problems of Democratic Transition and Consolidation: Southern Europe, South America, and Post-Communist Europe* (Baltimore: Johns Hopkins University Press, 1996), 55. Przeworski, however, expresses doubt about the nature of the previous regime as an explanatory variable: "I find surprisingly little evidence that the features of the 'new republic' do in fact correspond either to traits of the ancien régime or to modalities of transition." But he qualifies this statement, saying "the transitions we analyse are from authoritarianism, and the features of the ancien régime do shape their modalities and their directions. But the transitions are also to democracy, and the destination makes the paths converge." *Democracy and the Market,* 98–99.

35. According to Linz, "Reequilibration of a democracy is a political process that, after a crisis that has seriously threatened the continuity and stability of the basic democratic political mechanisms, results in their continued existence at the same or higher levels of democratic legitimacy, efficacy, and effectiveness. . . . The new regime might be established illegally, but it must be legitimated by the democratic process afterward, and above all, it must operate thereafter according to democratic rules." Juan J. Linz, *The Breakdown of Democratic Regimes: Crisis, Breakdown, and Reeequilibration* (Baltimore: Johns Hopkins University Press, 1978), 87.

36. Ahmad, *The Turkish Experiment,* 168–170.

37. Stepan, "Paths Toward Democratization," 75–78.

38. Przeworski, *Democracy and the Market,* 74–79.

39. Guillermo O'Donnell, *Modernization and Bureaucratic-Authoritarianism: Studies in South American Politics* (Berkeley: Institute of International Studies, University of California, 1973); also his "Tensions in the Bureaucratic-Authoritarian State and the Question of Democracy," in David Collier, ed., *The New Authoritarianism in Latin America*

(Princeton: Princeton University Press, 1979), 285–318; Carlos H. Weisman, *Reversal of Development in Argentina* (Princeton: Princeton University Press, 1987); Henri J. Barkey, *The State and the Industrialization Crisis in Turkey* (Boulder: Westview Press, 1990). To my knowledge, Barkey is the first author to give a convincing and comprehensive account of the 1980 military intervention in Turkey in terms of the exhaustion of ISI and the emergence of a BA regime. I had earlier pointed out, although briefly, the similarities between Latin American BAs and the Turkish NSC regime. See Ergun Özbudun, "Turkey: Crises, Interruptions, and Reequilibrations," in Larry Diamond, Juan J. Linz, and Seymour Martin Lipset, eds., *Politics in Developing Countries: Comparing Experiences with Democracy* (Boulder: Lynne Rienner, 1990), 213–214.

40. Barkey, *The State and the Industrialization Crisis in Turkey*, 173, 180. Interestingly, following the initiation of the January 24 measures, Bülent Ecevit, then leader of the RPP, had argued repeatedly that such measures could be implemented only by a Latin American–style authoritarian regime. See, for example, Cüneyt Arcayürek, *12 Eylüle Doğru Kosar Adım, Kasım 1979–Nisan 1980* (Running Toward 12 September), Vol. 9 (Ankara: Bilgi Yayınevi, 1986), 174–178.

41. Ahmad, *The Turkish Experiment*, 170–171.

42. Ibid., 179; also Metin Toker, *Demokrasimizin Ismet Pasalı Yılları: Yarı Silahlı, Yarı Külahlı Bir Ara Rejim, 1960–1961* (Our Years of Democracy with Ismet Pasha: A Half-Armed, Half-Civilian Interim Regime 1960–1961) (Ankara: Bilgi Yayınevi, 1991), 307–309.

43. Linz and Stepan, *The Breakdown of Democratic Regimes*, 4–5, 10.

44. Frey, *The Turkish Political Elite*, 196–197.

45. Ahmad, *The Turkish Experiment*, 30, 40.

46. Quote in Metin Toker, *Demokrasimizin Ismet Pasalı Yılları: DP Yokus Asagı, 1954–1957* (Our Years of Democracy with Ismet Pasha: DP Down Hill, 1954–1957) (Ankara: Bilgi Yayınevi, 1991), 26.

47. Ilter Turan, "Stages of Political Development in the Turkish Republic," in Ergun Özbudun, ed., *Perspectives on Democracy in Turkey* (Ankara: Turkish Political Science Association, 1988), 73. Ahmad argues in the same vein that the DP must be seen "as a movement embracing a variety of conflicting and contradictory interests united around a common goal, rather than as a political party with narrower interests and identification. The breadth of its interests was a great asset in opposition but proved to be a handicap in power." *The Turkish Experiment*, 77.

48. Ahmad observes that most Democrats harbored a deep fear of Inönü: "It was this factor, the Pasha factor . . . which bedevilled inter-party relations. . . . Inönü-phobia was based on the conviction that Ismet Pasha had not really accepted DP rule and was determined to undermine the Democrats at the first opportunity." *The Turkish Experiment*, 37.

49. Toker, *Yarı Silahlı, Yarı Külahlı Bir Ara Rejim*, 73–75.

50. Metin Toker, *Demokrasimizin Ismet Pasa'lı Yılları: Demokrasiden Darbeye, 1957–1960* (Our Years of Democracy with Ismet Pasha: From Democracy to the Coup, 1957–1960) (Ankara: Bilgi Yayınevi, 1991), 294–297.

51. On the concepts of disloyal, semiloyal, and loyal oppositions, see Linz, *The Breakdown of Democratic Regimes*, 27–38.

52. Toker, *Yarı Silahlı, Yarı Külahlı Bir Ara Rejim*, 21.

53. Toker, *Demokrasiden Darbeye,* 334, 341.

54. Ahmad, *The Turkish Experiment,* 292.

55. Ibid., 288–289.

56. Metin Toker, *Demokrasimizin Ismet Pasa'lı Yılları: Ismet Pasa'nın Son Yılları, 1965–1973* (Our Years of Democracy with Ismet Pasha: Last Years of Ismet Pasha, 1965–1973) (Ankara: Bilgi Yayınevi, 1993), 229.

57. Ahmad, *The Turkish Experiment,* 296; Ümit Cizre-Sakallıoglu, *AP-Ordu Iliskileri: Bir Ikilemin Anatomisi* (JP-Military Relationship: An Anatomy of a Dilemma) (Istanbul: Iletisim Yayınları, 1993), 111–119.

58. Linz, *The Breakdown of Democratic Regimes,* 32–33.

59. For the texts of the letters, see Cüneyt Arcayürek, *Müdahalenin Ayak Sesleri: 1978–1979* (The Footsteps of Intervention), Vol. 8 (Ankara: Bilgi Yayınevi, 1986), 76, 205; also his Volume 9, 65.

60. Cüneyt Arcayürek, *Demokrasinin Sonbaharı: 1977–1978* (The Autumn of Democracy), Vol. 7 (Ankara: Bilgi Yayınevi, 1985), 68, 456.

61. Arcayürek, Vol. 8, 175–177.

62. Ibid., 377–379.

63. See, for example, Arcayürek, Vol. 7, 165, 268–269, 425–426.

64. Quoted in Cüneyt Arcayürek, *Demokrasi Dur, 12 Eylül 1980: Nisan 1980–Eylül 1980* (Democracy Stop, 12 September 1980), Vol. 10 (Ankara: Bilgi Yayınevi, 1986), 85.

65. Quoted in ibid., 171–182.

66. *Hürriyet* (Istanbul daily), 21 March 1976.

67. *Cumhuriyet* (Istanbul daily), 25 December 1978, quoted in Cizre-Sakallıoglu, *AP-Ordu Iliskileri,* 144.

68. Quoted in Arcayürek, Vol. 10, 75, 124.

69. Ergun Özbudun, "The Turkish Party System: Institutionalization, Polarization, and Fragmentation," *Middle Eastern Studies* 17 (April 1981): 233. On the distinction between moderate and extreme multiparty systems, see Giovanni Sartori, *Parties and Party Systems: A Framework for Analysis* (Cambridge: Cambridge University Press, 1976), 139–140. Six parties were actually represented in the 1977 National Assembly, but two were not significant (or "relevant," in Sartori's terms) parties; the Republican Reliance Party had only three seats (soon reduced to one), and the Democratic Party had only one seat.

70. Arcayürek, Vol. 7, 65, 84, 93–97.

71. Ibid., 128–130.

72. Quoted in Cizre-Sakallıoglu, *AP-Ordu Iliskileri,* 216–217; National Security Council, Turkey, *12 September in Turkey: Before and After* (Ankara: General Secretariat of the National Security Council, 1982), 22.

73. Quoted in Arcayürek, Vol. 7, 261–262; Vol. 10, 48–50.

74. Arcayürek, Vol. 8, 25, 58.

75. Ibid., 307.

76. Ecevit elaborates on these proposals in a text he submitted to the martial law authorities after the 1980 intervention; the text is reproduced in Arcayürek, Vol. 10, 26–47. See also Ecevit's speech in the National Assembly on 22 July 1980, in ibid., 217–230.

77. Arcayürek, Vol. 9, 349.

78. Ibid., 325; Arcayürek, Vol. 8, 297.

79. Arcayürek, Vol. 10, 48–50; also Cizre-Sakallıoglu, *AP-Ordu Iliskileri,* 256.

80. Quoted in Arcayürek, Vol. 8, 270–271.

81. For the text of the letter, see Kenan Evren, *Kenan Evren'in Anıları,* Vol. 1 (Istanbul: Milliyet, 1990), 331–332; for an English translation, National Security Council, Turkey, *12 September in Turkey,* 160–161.

82. Arcayürek, Vol. 8, 280, 298; M. Ali Birand, *12 Eylül Saat 04.00* (Istanbul: Karacan, 1984), 206.

83. Cizre-Sakallıoglu, *AP-Ordu Iliskileri,* 124–129, particularly note 131.

84. Ibid., 131.

85. Linz, *The Breakdown of Democratic Regimes,* 30.

86. Cizre-Sakallıoglu, *AP-Ordu Iliskileri,* 146.

87. Ibid., 206; Arcayürek, Vol. 7, 491.

88. Cizre-Sakallıoglu, *AP-Ordu Iliskileri,* 233–239; for example, see Evren, *Kenan Evren'in Anıları,* 280–281, 345, 356, 427, 437; for Ecevit's views on such contacts, see Arcayürek, Vol. 8, 380–381. Demirel said similarly that "the soldiers cannot act alone. . . . There are civilian cadres who invite them. They existed in 12 March (1971) and they existed in 12 September (1980). This has become a profession for such civilian cadres" (quoted in Cizre-Sakallıoglu, 239).

89. Arcayürek, Vol. 8, 196; Vol. 9, 266–267.

3

The Politics of
Constitution Making

Constitution making, particularly during democratic transitions, is an excellent opportunity to build political institutions that will enjoy broad support from society and its political (and other) elites. Both the constitution-making process and its outcome (i.e., constitutional choices) are crucial aspects of the transition to and consolidation of democracy. Andrea Bonime-Blanc has argued that "constitution-making is at once the most varied and the most concentrated form of political activity during the transition. In it, political maneuvering, bargaining and negotiations take place and the political positions, agreements and disagreements between groups and leaders come to the fore. How the constitution drafters handle these issues may tell us crucial things about the transition and about the regime it leads to. The general character of both the process and its outcome may reveal clues about the new regime's potential for stability or instability."[1]

Put differently, the constitution-making process influences not only the mode of transition to democracy but also, and perhaps more importantly, prospects for the consolidation of democracy. I argue here that a consensual or consociational style of constitu-

tion making tends to increase considerably the chances for democratic consolidation.

Thus, it seems no accident that some of the most stable democratic constitutions of the post–World War II period—the best-
known examples are the German, Italian, and Spanish constitutions—are the products of broadly representative constituent
assemblies and a highly consensual style of constitution making.
In Italy, the Constituent Assembly elected in 1946 was dominated
by three major parties (the Christian Democrats, Socialists, and
Communists). Although the Christian Democrats were the
strongest party, the combined leftist vote (Communists and
Socialists) was greater than that of the Christian Democrats. The
latter group, however, occupied the central position in the political alignment and could usually produce a realignment of all
moderate and conservative forces around itself. Nevertheless, no
single coalition dominated Italian constitution making: "Instead,
fluid coalitions and consensual decision-making took place on an
issue by issue basis. . . . Even in the face of . . . potentially divisive issues, the process . . . was completed on a consensual basis
with most, if not all, political parties supporting the final version
of the new constitution."[2] The Italian constitution was highly
praised as "a true political monument." As Gianfranco Pasquino
observes, "So important was that period of collaboration, and so
celebrated were its results, that to this day the Communists have
stressed that they have little in common with the Christian
Democrats, except for the fact that they drafted the constitution
together."[3]

Similarly, the constitution-making process in post-Franco
Spain was dominated by an accommodational, consensual style,
which was encouraged by the results of the first free legislative
elections on 15 June 1977. The center-right Central Democratic
Union (UCD), under the leadership of Adolfo Suarez, emerged as
the largest party, with 34.7 percent of the vote and 165 of 350 (47.1
percent) Cortes seats. The Socialist Party received 29.2 percent of
the popular vote and 118 seats (33.7 percent). The two more ideological parties made disappointing showings; the Allianza
Popular (AP), with links to the Francoist past, received only 8.5
percent of the vote; and the Communists obtained 9.3 percent of
the vote. The new Cortes agreed at its first session that it would
meet as a Constituent Assembly. The results of the elections left

open the possibility of a rightist UCD-AD coalition in constitution making, but the UCD rarely resorted to this option. Although there were intermittent winning coalitions between the two parties, especially on moral issues, "such a coalition was in no way comprehensive or predominant. Instead of displaying polarization, the Spanish process may be a model of consensual politics where parties of widely differing ideologies, through accommodation, formed the predominant multilateral (consensual) coalition."[4]

Through painstaking, sometimes secret deliberations, compromises were reached between left and right on most fundamental constitutional issues. The consensual nature of the constitution-making process is reflected in the fact that the Congress and the Senate adopted the constitution almost unanimously, with only a few AP and Basque members voting against it or abstaining on 31 October 1978. This is also true of the constitutional referendum of 6 December 1978, at which the constitution was approved by 87.87 percent of the popular votes cast.[5]

At the other end of the spectrum, one can observe a confrontational or dissentious style of constitution making, the best examples of which are the 1946 French constitution and the 1976 Portuguese constitution. The French Constituent Assembly was dominated by three strong, disciplined, ideologically oriented parties (the Communists, the Socialists, and the Christian Democratic Popular Republican Movement) that failed to arrive at consensual solutions on a number of important constitutional issues. Consequently, the first draft of the constitution was rejected in the referendum, and the second was only narrowly adopted. Judging from the short life of the Fourth French Republic (1946–1958) and chronic government instability, this experience cannot be considered successful.

Similarly, the special circumstances that surrounded constitution making in post-Salazar Portugal affected both the style and the outcome of the constitution-making process. Because of a majority of the leftist parties (Socialists and Communists) in the Constituent Assembly and the influence of radical leftist officers, the process can be described as essentially dissentious rather than consensual: "Decision-making, coalitions and results were ideologically one-sided and achieved unilaterally . . . over the heads of the more centrist, second largest party, the People's Democratic

Party."[6] The 1976 constitution was full of ideological, dogmatic, and often purely rhetorical provisions concerning the socioeconomic system; many of these ideological statements were eliminated or revised in the 1982 constitutional revision. Thus, the full consolidation of democracy in Portugal required two extensive revisions (in 1982 and 1989) of the constitution.

In light of such comparative evidence, the Turkish experience in constitution making can be described as a series of missed opportunities to create political institutions based on broad consensus. None of the three republican constitutions (those of 1924, 1961, and 1982) or the Ottoman constitution of 1876 were written by a Constituent or a Legislative Assembly broadly representative of social forces or through a process of negotiations, bargaining, and compromise. Consequently, they all had weak political legitimacy.

THE 1924 CONSTITUTION

The first republican constitution in 1924 was developed by the Grand National Assembly (GNA) elected in 1923. The 1923 elections were strongly controlled and dominated by the Republican People's Party (RPP), newly organized by Mustafa Kemal and his supporters. None of the deputies who had opposed Kemal during the first legislative session of the Assembly (1920–1923) had been reelected. Thus, the new legislature was almost completely dominated by Kemalists, although a single-party system had not yet been consolidated when it debated the new constitution. Therefore, the constitutional debates took place in an atmosphere of relative freedom, even though the Assembly by no means represented all of the major forces in society.

Perhaps because of this atmosphere, the outcome of the process was a constitution that appeared democratic in both letter and spirit. The 1924 constitution maintained the Grand National Assembly as the supreme organ of the state, deviating only slightly from the assembly government model that had prevailed in the early 1920s. The constitution's main defect was its lack of a system of effective checks and balances to check the power of elected majorities. Therefore, when a de facto single-party regime was established in 1925, the constitution easily became an instrument of authoritarian government. The RPP leadership effectively controlled and monopolized nominations to the GNA, whose supreme powers came to be exercised by the party leadership and the executive. Hence, there was no need to adapt the constitution to fit the requirements of authoritarian government.

By the same token, no compelling need was felt to change the constitution to become more democratic when the RPP leadership introduced a multiparty democracy in 1945. The Turkish transition to democracy was accomplished with no constitutional revision and with only some changes in the election, press, and association laws. Because of an election law adopted in early 1950 that assured free and honest elections under judicial supervision, the opposition Democratic Party (DP) came to power in the elections of 14 May 1950.

The 1924 constitution remained unchanged during the ten-year period when the DP was in power. One may wonder why neither party attempted to introduce more effective constitutional checks and balances to lay the foundations for a more liberal and pluralistic democracy. The most plausible answer is that the RPP never thought seriously of losing power, and the DP, once in power, found that the unlimited majority rule the constitution provided served its own political advantage. Therefore, no meaningful constitutional dialogue took place between the government and the opposition parties either before or after the change of government in 1950.

The lack of such constitutional checks and balances turned out to be the main reason for the collapse of the first Turkish experiment with democracy. In the absence of effective legal guarantees of basic rights and judicial review of the constitutionality of laws, the DP government passed a series of laws that severely restricted the rights of the opposition, which, in turn, caused the opposition to develop a harsh attitude toward the government. The ensuing public unrest resulted in a military intervention on 27 May 1960, which overthrew the DP government and set up a temporary military regime.

THE 1961 CONSTITUTION

The 1960 coup was carried out by a group of middle-rank officers who, upon assuming power, organized into a revolutionary council called the National Unity Committee (NUC), chaired by General Cemal Gürsel, former commander of the army. From the beginning, the NUC declared its intention to create a new democratic constitution and return power to a freely elected civilian government. In spite of efforts by some NUC members to prolong military rule, the committee kept to its promise and relinquished power in 1961, following the parliamentary elections held under the new constitution and the electoral law.

The new constitution, however, was developed in less than fully democratic circumstances. The NUC remained as one of the chambers of the bicameral Constituent Assembly. Therefore, the military's influence was strongly felt in the making of the constitution. The civilian chamber (the House of Representatives) was also not fully representative. Nearly a third of its members were chosen by indirect elections; the rest were appointed or co-opted by the two opposition parties (the RPP and the Republican Peasant Nation Party), the head of the state (General Gürsel), the NUC, and such institutions as the judiciary, universities, bar associations, chambers of commerce and industry, trade unions, press associations, youth organizations, and so on. More important, supporters of the banned DP—roughly half of the Turkish electorate—had no representation in the Constituent Assembly.

The Constituent Assembly was thus dominated largely by the state elites (the military, the bureaucracy, and university professors) and the RPP, the principal spokesperson of those elites. Consequently, the 1961 constitution, adopted by the Assembly and ratified by a majority of 61.7 percent of the popular vote, reflected the basic political values and interests of the state elites. Thus, on the one hand, the constitution greatly expanded civil liberties and granted extensive social rights for citizens; on the other hand, it reflected a distrust of politicians and elective assemblies by creating an effective system of checks and balances to limit the power of those elected organs. These checks included the introduction of judicial review of the constitutionality of laws; strengthening the administrative courts, with review powers over all executive agencies; full independence for the judiciary; creation of a second chamber of the Legislative Assembly; improved job security for civil servants, especially judges; and granting substantial administrative autonomy to certain public agencies, such as the universities and the Radio and Television Corporation. It was hoped that the power of the elected assemblies would be effectively balanced by judicial and other bureaucratic agencies and that the newly expanded civil liberties and social rights would ensure the gradual development of a genuinely pluralistic and democratic society.

With regard to the regulation of socioeconomic issues, the majority in the Constituent Assembly interpreted the old Kemalist notion of etatism in a more leftist and ideological way. Consequently, many programmatic and ideological statements were incorporated into the constitution. Thus, the state was entrusted with economic, social, and cultural planning; land reform; health care and housing; social security organizations; helping to assure full employment; and similar tasks. The state was also empowered to force private enterprises to act "in accordance with the requirements of national economy and with social objectives" (Article 49).

Neither the circumstances of its creation nor its substance allowed the 1961 constitution to be accepted by the majority of Turkish society. Former Democrats, in part because they had been totally excluded from the constitution-making process, voted against it in the constitutional referendum on 9 July 1961. The Justice Party (JP), which came to power in 1965 as the established heir of the banned DP, was ambivalent toward the constitution. The JP was careful to operate within the limits of the constitution but criticized those aspects that, in its view, gave bureaucratic and judicial agencies excessive powers. JP leaders often expressed the view that the constitution created an "ungovernable" political system, and they demanded a stronger executive. They were uncomfortable with the extensive social rights recognized by the constitution, as well as its other left-leaning provisions.

The views of Celal Bayar, deposed president of the republic under the DP regime, were both more systematic and extreme than those of the JP. Bayar argued that the 1924 constitution was more in accordance with the Kemalist notion of unconditional sovereignty because it concentrated all power in the Grand National Assembly as the sole representative of the Turkish nation. The 1961 constitution introduced new partners—the army and intellectuals—into the exercise of national sovereignty. Thus, it reflected a distrust of elected assemblies and represented a return to the Ottoman notion of a tripartite (palace, army, and religious scholars) government.[7] No doubt, such negative views of the 1961 constitution were also motivated in part by the fact that the DP-JP had been the "natural" majority party in the 1950s and 1960s and was therefore resentful of bureaucratic limitations on the power of elected assemblies.

THE 1971 AND 1973 CONSTITUTIONAL REVISIONS

The tension between state elites and the JP as the principal representative of political elites tended to decrease in the late 1960s. The JP government treated the military with much greater care and respect than the DP government had. The National Security Council, an advisory body created by the 1961 constitution and composed of some ministers and the highest commanders of the armed forces, gave the military a legitimate voice in the formulation of national security policies. The Grand National Assembly's choice of former military commanders as president of the republic (General Gürsel in 1961 and General Cevdet Sunay in 1966) also reassured most officers. Finally, salaries and other benefits for officers improved greatly in the 1960s.

Although a strong radical faction within the armed forces was still unhappy with the JP government and its basically conservative policies, that group's conspiratorial activities failed to gain the support of the top military leadership. The radical officers, frustrated by the successive JP electoral victories, aimed to establish a longer-term military regime to carry out radical social reforms; in fact, the military memorandum of 12 March 1971 that forced the JP government to resign was a last-minute move by top military commanders to forestall a radical coup. In the days following, most radical officers were summarily retired or dismissed, thereby strengthening the position of the more conservative military leaders. The so-called 12 March regime did not go as far as dissolving the parliament and assuming power directly. Instead, it urged the formation of an above-party, or technocratic, government under veteran RPP politician Nihat Erim.

The policies of the nonparty government, with strong behind-the-scenes support from the military, were more in line with the JP's conservative philosophy. This fact is also evident in the extensive 1971 and 1973 constitutional amendments, which incorporated most of the JP's positions into the constitution. The amendments can be grouped into three categories: (1) curtailing certain civil liberties in conjunction with restrictions of the review power of the courts; (2) strengthening the executive, particularly by allowing the GNA to grant it law-making powers; (3) increasing the institutional autonomy of the military by excluding it from review by civilian administrative courts and the Court of Account.

With the possible exception of the last item, the amendments were in accordance with the JP's constitutional thesis, and JP and other conservative deputies readily voted in favor. To obtain the two-thirds majority required for constitutional change, pressure was apparently exerted on the RPP leadership and its deputies. The threat of dissolution of the parliament, expressed clearly in the 12 March memorandum, and the highly repressive atmosphere produced by the martial law regime also weakened and discouraged the opposition.[8] Thus, once again constitutional change was accomplished by highly dissentious methods, with no process of genuine negotiation and compromise among political parties. One side imposed its favored solutions on the other, taking advantage of the threat of force by the military.

THE 1982 CONSTITUTION

The making of the 1982 constitution was another missed opportunity to create political institutions with broad consensus. Although the National Security Council (NSC) (composed of the five highest-ranking generals in the Turkish armed forces) that took over the government on 12 September 1980 made it clear that it intended eventually to return power to democratically elected civilian authorities, it made it equally clear that it did not intend to return to the status quo ante. Rather, the council intended a major restructuring of Turkish democracy to prevent a recurrence of the political polarization, violence, and deadlock that had afflicted the country in the late 1970s.

This restructuring was done by a Constituent Assembly created by the NSC. As in the case of the 1960–1961 Constituent Assembly, the structure was bicameral, one chamber of which was the NSC itself. Important differences were found between this Constituent Assembly and its predecessor, however. In the present case, the civilian chamber (the Consultative Assembly) was even less representative than the House of Representatives of the 1960–1961 period. Whereas the latter included representatives of the two opposition parties and various other institutions, all members of the former were appointed by the NSC. Furthermore, no political party members were eligible to become members of the Consultative Assembly. Consequently, the state elites had even more weight in the Consultative Assembly than they had in the House of Representatives.

Second, the Consultative Assembly had much less power vis-à-vis the NSC than the House of Representatives had enjoyed vis-à-vis the NUC. In the latter case, the two chambers had roughly equal powers regarding the adoption of the constitution and other laws; in the former, the NSC kept the final say. In other words, the NSC had the absolute power to amend or reject the constitutional draft prepared by the Consultative Assembly, with no machinery envisaged to resolve the differences between the two chambers.

Third, whereas the 1961 constitutional referendum took place in a reasonably free atmosphere and those who opposed the constitution (particularly the JP) were able to propagate their views, the 1982 referendum followed a one-sided campaign conducted by General Kenan Evren, the head of state and chair of the NSC. An NSC decree prohibited the expression of any views intended to influence voters' decisions and banned criticism of the transitional articles of the constitution or of speeches Evren made in his pro-constitution campaign.

Finally, the 1982 constitutional referendum was combined with the election of the president of the republic. A "yes" vote for the constitution was also an endorsement of the presidency of Evren (the sole candidate) for a seven-year period. Under these circumstances, the constitution was approved on 7 November 1982 by 91.37 percent of voters.

The 1982 constitution—again reflecting the values and interests of state elites—was even less trustful than its predecessor of the "national will," elected assemblies, political parties, politicians, and all other civil society institutions such as trade unions, professional organizations, and voluntary associations. Trade unions were weakened, and the freedom of association was severely restricted. No cooperation was allowed between political parties on the one hand and unions, professional organizations, foundations, associations, and cooperative societies on the other. If the 1982 constitution somewhat curbed the review powers of the judiciary and the autonomy of universities, this was not intended to strengthen elected assemblies and responsible governments at the expense of bureaucratic agencies. Rather, the intent was to create a strong presidency, which the makers of the 1982 constitution (almost all of whom were military officers and civilian bureaucrats) assumed would long be controlled by the military. Indeed, Evren, the leader of the 1980 coup, served as president until November 1989.

A major difference between the development of the 1961 and 1982 constitutions is that in the latter case the military no longer trusted civilian bureaucratic agencies, which it perceived as highly fragmented, infiltrated by political parties, and vulnerable to radical political ideas. Therefore, the president of the republic was given important substantive powers in appointing high-court judges and university administrators, the two areas the military considered particularly sensitive. In short, the 1982 constitution was designed to maintain the military as the ultimate guardian and arbiter of the political system through a strengthened presidency and National Security Council.

This emphasis on strengthening the presidency led to different interpretations of the system of government created by the 1982 constitution. Some observers perceived it as a presidential or semipresidential system. Another view held that the constitution provided two alternative models of government. If the system functioned normally (i.e., without a crisis) it would be closer to a parliamentary government in which the prime minister, not the president of the republic, would predominate; this is precisely what happened under the premiership of Turgut Özal (1983–1989). If, on the other hand, the party system failed to avoid or resolve crises, then "the substitute power" of the president (or of the state apparatus as personified by the president) would grow, and the system would become closer to presidentialism.[9] According to a third view, the logic of the 1982 constitution dictated parliamentarism, even though the president was more powerful than most heads of state in parliamentary systems.

Therefore, borrowing a French term, *parlementarisme attenué*, the 1982 constitution's system of government can best be described as a modified or weakened form of parliamentarism.[10] This reading of the constitution appears to be more consistent with constitutional practice as it has evolved since the retransition to democracy in 1983. The system functioned essentially as a parliamentary government not only when Özal was both prime minister and leader of the majority party but also during the premierships of Mesut Yılmaz, Süleyman Demirel, and Tansu Çiller.[11]

DEBATES ON CONSTITUTIONAL CHANGE SINCE 1983

The 1982 constitution—written under the aegis of the military, excluding all political parties and other institutions of civil society, and approved by a highly dubious referendum—became a matter of public debate and contestation almost from its adoption. The Motherland Party (MP), however, which was the majority party between November 1983 and October 1991, did not seem to favor major constitutional revisions. Özal often expressed the view that the new institutions created by the 1982 constitution should be given a chance to function for a time before amendments could seriously be considered. Also underlying this position was Özal's desire to avoid an open confrontation with President Evren, who had declared himself the "guarantor" of the 1982 constitution. More generally, Özal often stated that the 1982 constitution was exceedingly detailed and that its rigidity obstructed government dynamism. In this context, he proposed a constitution that would consist only of a bill of rights. The MP leaders also spoke from time to time in favor of a constitutional amendment to transform the system of government into a semipresidential one in which the president of the republic would be directly elected by the people and would have increased powers. No clear party policy has evolved on any of these points, however, and none of these proposals have been energetically pursued.

During the 1983–1991 period, the two major opposition parties (the Social Democratic Populist Party [SDPP] and the True Path Party [TPP]) both produced highly detailed constitutional projects. The SDPP project envisaged a classical parliamentary system in which the president of the republic would be elected by a three-fifths majority of the parliament (to assure his or her impartiality) and would have very limited powers. The SDPP plan also emphasized strengthening the independence of the judiciary, increasing the autonomy of universities, and lifting restrictions on the political activities of trade unions and other civil society institutions. In a sense, the SDPP project meant a return to the basic features of the 1961 constitution.

The TPP project envisaged a more radical departure from the Turkish constitutional tradition by proposing a semipresidential system, clearly inspired by the French Fifth Republic model. The president of the republic would be elected by the people in a two-ballot system and would have the power to dissolve the Assembly at his or her initiative, to submit laws to referendum, to return laws to the Assembly for reconsideration (in which case the latter could override the presidential veto not by a simple majority but by an absolute majority of its full membership), and to determine the fundamental principles of national security and foreign policies. The president would also be head of the Supreme Council of the Judiciary and would therefore have the power to veto nominations for judges. The TPP plan also envisaged removing certain restrictions on civil liberties and on the political activities of civil society institutions such as trade unions and voluntary associations.[12]

The only significant amendment to the constitution during the years of the MP government was adopted by Law 3261, dated 18 May 1987. Except for two relatively minor and noncontroversial changes that lowered the voting age from twenty-one to twenty and increased the number of deputies from 400 to 450, the amendment involved a change in the amendment procedure to make constitutional change somewhat easier and the repeal of provisional Article 4, which had banned political activities by former political party leaders. The amended Article 175 provides for two methods of amendment. One requires a less stringent majority for the adoption of constitutional changes: if the Turkish Grand National Assembly (TGNA) passes an amendment by a majority greater than three-fifths but less than two-thirds of its full membership, such a bill can become a constitutional amendment, provided it is approved by popular referendum. In such cases, constitutional referendum is mandatory if the president does not return the bill to the Assembly for reconsideration. If he or she does so, the amendment procedure becomes identical to the second method: if a proposed amendment is adopted by the Assembly by a two-thirds majority of its full membership, the president has the power to submit it to referendum. In this case, referendum is optional, unlike the first method of amendment.

In short, the 1987 amendment made the constitution somewhat more flexible than it had been and increased popular control over constitutional change by broadening the scope of referendum, in which a simple majority of the total number of valid votes cast is sufficient to amend. Prime Minister Özal defended the change in the amendment procedure, pointing out that in the past the failure of political parties to agree on a constitutional amendment to obtain the required two-thirds majority of the parliament led to deadlocks in the political system; hence, constitutional changes had been possible only during periods of military takeover. Therefore, he added, constitutional change should be facilitated by giving the people the final word in cases of a parliamentary deadlock.[13]

The second important constitutional amendment created by Law 3261 was the repeal of the ban on political activities of former party leaders. Although no political party represented in the Assembly made a statement favoring continuation of the ban, the MP insisted that the repeal must be submitted to a referendum. The opposition parties argued that the ban should be repealed by the parliament alone and that a referendum was both unnecessary and undemocratic. The fundamental political rights of individuals, the opposition insisted, should not be put to a referendum. In the end, however, the TPP deputies, eager for an end to the ban, joined the MP majority in favor of conditional repeal of the ban. The referendum, held on 6 September 1987, approved the repeal by a hairbreadth majority (50.1 percent). Although all opposition parties supported the repeal in the referendum campaign, the MP opposed it.

In 1988 an attempt was made to change Article 127 of the constitution concerning local elections under the new amendment procedure. The amendment, passed by the Assembly by more than a three-fifths but less than a two-thirds majority, was automatically submitted to referendum and was rejected by a popular majority of 65 percent. The results of these two referenda suggest that the majority of voters tend to vote on the basis of party loyalty rather than on the merits of the proposed constitutional amendment.

The 20 October 1991 elections ended the MP government and brought to power a coalition government of the TPP and the SDPP. Both parties had been highly critical of the 1982 constitution, and both had promised sweeping constitutional changes in their election campaigns; therefore, one would have expected much greater constitutional change, despite the fact that the combined parliamentary strength of the two parties fell short of the required two-thirds majority and even of a three-fifths majority. The parliamentary arithmetic made it necessary to obtain the support of the MP, the major opposition party, or of all minor opposition parties to achieve constitutional change.

Negotiations took place between the two coalition partners to find common ground for proposing constitutional amendments with the expectation that other parties would lend their support. In principle, the SDPP favored an entirely new constitution. Given the practical difficulty of accomplishing that aim, it presented a draft in which seventy-five articles of the 1982 constitution were retained, ninety-six articles were revised, twenty-three articles were abolished, and one new article was drafted.[14] The TPP did not present a full draft but proposed changes in around thirty articles.[15] The TPP and the SDPP agreed on the texts of thirteen articles: Article 13 (restrictions on fundamental rights and freedoms), Article 26 (freedom of expression), Article 28 (freedom of the press), Article 30 (protection of printing facilities), Article 33 (freedom of association), Article 34 (freedom of assembly), Article 67 (right to vote), Article 68 (political parties), Article 69 (rules governing the activities of political parties), Article 76 (eligibility to become a member of parliament), Article 81 (the oath of the members of parliament), Article 92 (authorization of the use of armed forces), and Article 133 (radio and television broadcasts). The two also agreed on the repeal of the provisional articles and agreed in principle on a number of other points.[16]

At this point, Hüsamettin Cindoruk, speaker of the Grand National Assembly, invited all parties represented in the Assembly to present their views on the constitution. Party leaders met, with Cindoruk presiding, to obtain agreement on those articles that could muster the necessary two-thirds majority. The work of the interparty committee was interrupted for a long period, however, because of political circumstances including the death of President Özal, the election of Demirel as president of the republic, Tansu Çiller's rise to prime minister and leader of the TPP, and the local elections of March 1994. Only the amendment concerning Article 133 was separated from the others because of its special urgency and was approved by a two-thirds majority of the Assembly. Thus, state monopoly over radio and television broadcasts was abolished.

The interparty committee resumed its work in spring 1994, again at the initiative of Speaker of the Assembly Cindoruk. After painful and protracted negotiations, an amendment proposal—signed by 301 deputies (more than the two-thirds majority needed to change the constitution without a referendum) including the parliamentary group leaders of the TPP, the MP, and the SDPP (now the Republican People's Party [RPP])—was submitted to the TGNA on 15 January 1995. This proposal involved changes to the preamble and twenty articles of the constitution, the most important of which were these: The first two paragraphs of the preamble underlining the legitimacy of the 1980 military intervention were to be repealed; the ban on the political activities of trade unions, associations, foundations, and public professional organizations and on political cooperation between such civil society institutions and political parties was to be abolished; public employees were to be given the right to unionize and—in a manner to be regulated by law—the rights to strike and to conclude collective agreements; government controls over the activities of associations, trade unions, and public professional organizations were to be relaxed; the voting age would be lowered to eighteen (from nineteen) and the age of eligibility for parliament to twenty-five (from thirty); instructors and students in institutions of higher learning were to be allowed to become members of political parties; the age for party membership was to be lowered from twenty-one to eighteen; political parties were to be permitted to establish women's and youth branches, foundations, and organizations in foreign countries; the circumstances under which TGNA membership could be lost were to become more liberal; and the provisional Article 15 of the constitution was to be amended to permit judicial review of the constitutionality of laws passed during NSC rule.

The amendment proposal was based on an agreement among the three major parties—the TPP, the MP, and the RPP—and was signed by deputies of those parties. The Welfare Party (WP) had insisted during the interparty negotiations that the package must include the repeal of the last paragraph of Article 24 of the constitution, which stated that "no one shall exploit or abuse religion or religious feelings, or things deemed sacred by religion in any manner whatsoever, for the purpose of personal or political interest or influence, or for even partially basing the fundamental social, economic, political, and legal order of the State on religious rules." The WP believed this paragraph was the source of discriminatory and "oppressive" practices against devout Muslims, including the ban on wearing turbans and growing beards for students, civil servants, and even such free professionals as lawyers and engineers. The WP made it clear that it would not vote for any constitutional amendment that did not include the repeal of this paragraph.[17]

In contrast to the total WP refusal to support the constitutional amendments, the smaller parties represented in the TGNA were much more constructive. Bülent Ecevit, leader of the Democratic Left Party (DLP), reiterated several times that his party considered some of the proposed amendments insufficient but that all ten DLP deputies would vote in favor—albeit sometimes unhappily—if the amendments constituted even the smallest steps toward a true democracy.[18] Similar attitudes were displayed by the Nationalist Action Party (NAP).[19]

The Constitutional Committee of the TGNA combined the amendment proposal, signed by 301 deputies, with two other, more specific proposals. One was submitted by Günes Müftüoglu (of the TPP) and 170 other deputies to allow the TGNA to postpone or anticipate local elections. The other was submitted by Cemal Tercan (of the TPP) and 153 colleagues to make parliamentary status compatible with membership in the executive boards of trade unions and public professional organizations.

The proposed texts were changed somewhat by the Constitutional Committee, generally in a more conservative direction, and debate on them began in the plenary session of the TGNA on 14 June 1995. The fact that 301 deputies from three major parties had already signed the proposals and that two minor parties (the DLP and the NAP) also supported them gave the impression that the WP would be alone in opposition and that the amendments would easily pass. Early in the plenary debates, however, it became apparent that this would not be the case. In the first reading, the vote on the entire amendment bill was 298 in favor and 86 opposed, with 4 abstentions—sufficient to continue debates on individual articles but short of the two-thirds majority (300 votes) required for the amendment to be adopted without a referendum. Only seven of the individual articles were adopted by the required three-fifths majority (270 votes), and none received a two-thirds majority. Fifteen articles failed to receive even a three-fifths majority.[20]

There were several reasons for this impasse. First, even though the WP parliamentary group had only forty members, many religiously conservative members of the TPP and the MP sympathized with the WP position and did not vote for the amendments. Second, the compromise between the two government partners (the TPP and the RPP) on the unionization of public employees was a thin one. A majority of TPP deputies, particularly the influential spokesman of the Constitutional Committee, Coskun Kırca, would not consider unionization rights if they included the rights to strike and to conclude collective agreements. For the RPP, these rights constituted the most essential part of the package. A compromise solution proposed by the RPP and supported by the MP, the WP, and the small parties that recognized such rights in the constitution but left their detailed definition and exceptions to ordinary legislation could not muster the necessary three-fifths majority. Third, a large number of MP deputies gave lukewarm support to the amendments for fear Prime Minister Çiller would try to monopolize the credit for changing the constitution.[21]

Faced with this deadlock, the Constitutional Committee withdrew some of the proposed amendments, debates were postponed, and a few rounds of talks took place among party leaders—with the exception of Necmettin Erbakan, the WP leader, who was determined to block constitutional change. Prior to the second reading, the speaker of the TGNA prepared a legal opinion according to which all articles would be voted on in the second reading, regardless of the number of votes they had received in the first reading; articles that received fewer than 270 votes (three-fifths) in the second reading would be rejected; if the amendment bill was approved in its entirety by a two-thirds majority (300 or more votes), no referendum would be needed for any of its articles, even if they received between 270 and 300 votes; if the entire bill was approved with a majority of 270 to 300 votes, all articles would be submitted to referendum regardless of the number of votes they received in the second reading. These opinions, the constitutionality of which is highly doubtful, were voted on and approved by the Assembly.[22]

The second reading went somewhat more smoothly than the first as a result of compromises reached among party leaders. Consequently, fifteen articles were adopted (seven by more than 300 votes and eight by a majority of 270 to 300 votes) and six articles were rejected, having failed to receive a three-fifths majority. In the final vote on the entire bill on 23 July, there were 360 votes in favor and 32 opposed. Therefore, in accordance with the procedural resolution mentioned earlier, all fifteen articles were considered to be definitively adopted without the need for a mandatory popular referendum.

The most important amendments can be summarized as follows: They repealed the two paragraphs of the preamble referring to the necessity and legitimacy of the 1980 military intervention. They repealed the bans on political activities of trade unions, associations, foundations, cooperatives, and public professional organizations and allowed political cooperation between political parties and these civil society institutions. They lowered the voting age to eighteen, increased the number of TGNA members to 550 (from 450), gave Turkish citizens living abroad the right to vote, recognized the right to unionize (but not the right to strike or to conclude collective agreements) for public employees, allowed university instructors and students to become members of political parties, lowered the age of party membership from twenty-one to eighteen, and permitted political parties to establish women's and youth branches, foundations, and organizations in foreign countries.

Suspension of activities of associations and public professional organizations by order of an administrative authority was made more difficult; such orders are to be submitted to the review of the competent judge within twenty-four hours and must be decided on by the judge within forty-eight hours or they automatically cease to be effective. The circumstances under which parliamentary membership is lost were also changed so that changing one's political party would no longer be a cause for loss of membership. Similarly, if a political party is outlawed by the

Constitutional Court because of its anticonstitutional activities, only those members of parliament who caused such a decision by their own words or deeds would lose their membership; the status of other party deputies would remain unaffected.

Amendments rejected included those that would have given public employees the rights to strike and to conclude collective agreements, that lowered the age of eligibility for parliament to twenty-five (from thirty), that allowed trade union and professional organization officials to sit in parliament, and that permitted judicial review of the constitutionality of laws passed during National Security Council rule. The last item is especially interesting in that during the first and second readings spokespersons from all parties spoke very strongly in favor of the amendment; yet it received only 200 "yes" votes against 184 rejections and 5 abstentions.[23] Thus, the National Assembly failed to remove an important relic that remained from the military government.

The 1995 constitutional amendments fell far short of popular expectations. Although during the Assembly debates all party spokespersons saw this as a historical opportunity to allow a freely elected civilian parliament to make major democratizing changes to the constitution, the end result did not live up to this hope. The amendments related mostly to the political participation dimension of the constitution and were useful in that regard, but they brought about no improvements in the rule of law and protection of fundamental rights and liberties. Nevertheless, the amendments provided an example, albeit a limited one, of interparty cooperation—which is not a distinguishing mark of Turkish politics.

*   *   *

The history of constitution making in Turkey described here suggests that none of the three republican constitutions was made by a broadly representative Constituent Assembly through a process of negotiations, bargaining, and compromise. In all three cases, as well as in the extensive constitutional revisions in 1971 and 1973, the influence of state elites was predominant in constitution making, and the role of civil society institutions was correspondingly negligible. Therefore, all three constitutions had weak political legitimacy, and judged by the frequency of military intervention in politics, none produced a fully consolidated democratic regime.

Clearly, the 1982 constitution, a product of a highly unrepresentative process, has not found acceptance in the most important political sectors of Turkish society. All political parties, no matter what their differences, seem to favor changing the constitution in a more liberal, pluralistic, and participatory direction. This is also the position taken by other major civil society institutions, such as the Turkish Industrialists' and Businessmen's Association (TÜSIAD), the Turkish Confederation of Employers' Unions, the Press Council, and the two major trade unions, Türk-Is and Hak-Is.[24] With regard to acceptance of present political institutions by the general public, scant public opinion data exist. A study carried out in 1990–1991, however, showed that 50.3 percent of Turkish respondents had little or no trust in the Turkish political system, and 41.9 percent had little or no trust in the Grand National Assembly. Compared with the much higher levels of trust for other social institutions (91.4 percent of respondents had high or moderate trust in the armed forces, 67.1 percent in religious institutions, 66.8 percent in the education system, and 63.4 percent in the police), these findings are interesting and may give rise to concern.[25]

Explaining this paradox is not easy. Perhaps one reason it exists is the weakness of linkages between political parties and other civil society institutions. These linkages, which were never strong, were further and deliberately weakened by the 1982 constitution, resulting in increased volatility of party votes (i.e., percentage changes in party votes from one election to the next) and the relative insulation of political parties from societal demands and pressures. Recent interparty maneuverings over constitutional change suggest that parties tend to see such change as an essentially political game in which they are reluctant to collaborate with their adversaries unless their own favorite items are included in the package.

NOTES

1. Andrea Bonime-Blanc, *Spain's Transition to Democracy: The Politics of Constitution-Making* (Boulder: Westview Press, 1987), 13.
2. Ibid., 121.

3. Gianfranco Pasquino, "The Demise of the First Fascist Regime and Italy's Transition to Democracy: 1943–1948," in Guillermo O'Donnell, Philippe C. Schmitter, and Laurence Whitehead, eds., *Transitions from Authoritarian Rule: Southern Europe* (Baltimore: Johns Hopkins University Press, 1986), 64.

4. Bonime-Blanc, *Spain's Transition to Democracy,* 143, also 54–55.

5. Ibid., 39–42, 59–62; also Jose Maria Maravall and Julian Santamaria, "Political Change in Spain and the Prospects for Democracy," in Guillermo O'Donnell, Philippe C. Schmitter, and Laurence Whitehead, eds., *Transitions from Authoritarian Rule: Southern Europe* (Baltimore: Johns Hopkins University Press, 1986), 87–89.

6. Bonime-Blanc, *Spain's Transition to Democracy,* 119, 122.

7. Bülent Tanör, *Iki Anayasa: 1961 ve 1982* (The Two Constitutions: 1961 and 1982) (Istanbul: Beta, 1986), 29–37, 61–67.

8. Ibid., 39–60.

9. Bakır Çaglar, "Anayasa Mahkemesi Kararlarında Demokrasi" (Democracy in Constitutional Court Decisions), in *Anayasa Yargısı,* Vol. 7 (Ankara: Anayasa Mahkemesi Yayınları, 1990), 103–110.

10. Ergun Özbudun, *Türk Anayasa Hukuku* (Turkish Constitutional Law) (Ankara: Yetkin Yayınları, 1993), 307–312.

11. See also Metin Heper, "The Executive in the Third Turkish Republic," *Governance* 3 (1990): 299–319.

12. *Isleyen Rejim, Isleyen Devlet* (Functioning Regime, Functioning State), paper prepared by Necmettin Cevheri, member of the Central Executive Committee of the True Path Party (Ankara, 1991).

13. *TBMM Tutanak Dergisi* (Verbatim Report of the TGNA Debates), Term 17, Legislative Year 4, Vol. 40, Session 102, 13 May 1987, 302.

14. *TBMM'de Temsil Edilen Siyasi Partilerce TBMM Baskanlığına Sunulan Anayasa Degisikligi Konusundaki Görüs ve Önerileri* (The Views and Proposals of Political Parties Represented in the TGNA Concerning Constitutional Amendments, as Presented to the Speaker of the TGNA) (Ankara: TGNA Baskanligi, March 1993), 122–173.

15. Ibid., 37–38.

16. *TBMM'de Temsil Edilen Siyasi Partilerin Anayasa Degisikligi Tekliflerinin Karsılastırmalı Metinleri* (Comparative Texts of the Proposals of Political Parties Represented in the TGNA Concerning Constitutional Amendments) (Ankara: TBMM Baskanlığı, March 1993), esp. xi–xiv.

17. See, for example, the speech by Sevket Kazan, leader of the WP parliamentary group, during the TGNA debates on constitutional amendment; *TBMM Tutanak Dergisi,* Term 19, Legislative Year 4, Vol. 88, Session 123, 14 June 1995, 376–382. Abdullah Gül, deputy from the WP, said that "while we have this opportunity let us make a democratic constitution similar to those of the European countries, a constitution that is not afraid of its own people, of its own nation, respectful of the tradition, identity, culture, and religion of its nation" (409–413).

18. Ibid., Term 19, Legislative Year 4, Vol. 89, Session 128, 23 June 1995, 485; Term 19, Legislative Year 4, Vol. 91, Session 136, 7 July 1995, 37–38.

19. NAP deputy Mustafa Dagci stated that even though some did not quite agree with their views, all seventeen NAP deputies voted "yes" for all of the amendments, since the amendments represented an

improvement over the existing provisions and the people expected the TGNA to pass them. He went on to say that it was important for the future consolidation of democracy to show that the constitution could be amended by freely elected civilian politicians; ibid., Term 19, Legislative Year 4, Vol. 89, Session 127, 22 June 1995, 317.

20. The amendment procedure is discussed earlier in this chapter.

21. Ecevit's remarks on the impasse are pertinent: "A very important duty falls upon the TGNA. If the TGNA had been able to realize at least some of the democratizing changes expected by the society—and there is still this chance—it would have gained great respect and proved the maturity of Turkish democracy. But unfortunately, constitutional debates seem to be at an impasse now. The TGNA is facing the danger of falling prey to itself, not to outside pressures and threats. . . . The truth is that the TPP, the RPP, and the MP got involved in an obstinate fight, losing sight of the fact that this was a regime issue. Not only disagreements among these parties but also internal conflicts within each of them prevented a compromise and led to this deadlock"; *TBMM Tutanak Dergisi*, Term 19, Legislative Year 4, Vol. 91, Session 136, 7 July 1995, 37–38.

22. For the text of the speaker's opinion, see ibid., Term 19, Legislative Year 4, Vol. 90, Session 134, 5 July 1995, 559. In the debates on this opinion, only the WP spokespersons pointed out, in my view correctly, the unconstitutionality of this procedure (559–567). Two readings are required for constitutional amendments not to facilitate the amendments but to make them more difficult compared with ordinary laws; therefore, articles that received less than the qualified majority in the first reading should be considered rejected and not be voted on in the second reading. I think, furthermore, that every article of constitutional amendments should be treated as a separate unit and not be tied to the vote on the entire bill. The issue of constitutionality was not raised before the Constitutional Court, since the WP was far short of the numbers (one-fifth of total deputies) necessary to go to the court. Thus, ironically, certain democratizing changes to the constitution were accomplished through a procedure whose constitutionality is dubious.

23. For the Assembly debates on this amendment, see ibid., Term 19, Legislative Year 4, Vol. 90, Session 132, 29 June 1995, 274–299, and Vol. 93, Session 146, 22 July 1995, 280–294.

24. *TBMM Baskanlıgına Bazı Kurum ve Kuruluslarca Verilmis ve Ayrıca TBMM'deki Siyasi Partilerin Anayasa Degisikligine Iliskin Hazırlık Çalısmaları ve Taslak Metinler* (Preparatory Studies and Draft Texts Concerning Constitutional Amendments, as Presented to the Speaker of the TGNA by Certain Institutions and Associations and by Political Parties Represented in the TGNA) (Ankara: TBMM Baskanlıgı, 22 February 1993), 5–230.

25. *Türk Toplumunun Degerleri* (The Values of Turkish Society) (Istanbul: TÜSIAD, 1991), 22–23.

4

Parties and the Party System

THE PARTY SYSTEM: DEINSTITUTIONALIZATION, FRAGMENTATION, AND POLARIZATION

Turkey is distinguished from many new democracies by the relatively high institutionalization of its political parties. Commenting on Turkish politics in the 1950s, Frederick Frey argued that "Turkish politics are party politics. . . . Within the power structure of Turkish society, the political party is the main unofficial link between the government and the larger, extragovernmental groups of people. . . . It is perhaps in this respect above all—the existence of extensive, powerful, highly organized, grass roots parties—that Turkey differs institutionally from the other Middle Eastern nations with whom we frequently compare her."[1] Yet, as this chapter makes clear, parties and the party system in Turkey have been experiencing a protracted process of institutional decay since the 1970s, with growing fragmentation, ideological polarization, and electoral volatility in the party system and declining organizational capacity of, public support for, and identification with individual parties.

In the next section I discuss the common organizational characteristics of Turkish political parties, arguing that those parties have not generally displayed mass party characteristics but rather have combined the features of cadre, catchall, and cartel parties. In the following sections, I discuss the social, ideological, and organizational characteristics of the main Turkish parties (the Welfare Party, the Motherland Party, the True Path Party, the Democratic Left Party, and the Republican People's Party, with a brief section on minor parties).

Between 1946 and 1960, the Turkish party system displayed the characteristics of a typical two-party system; the two main contenders were the Republican People's Party (RPP) and the Democratic Party (DP). In the 1961 elections that followed the 1960 military intervention, no party obtained a parliamentary majority because of the fragmentation of the former DP votes (the DP was banned by the military regime) among three parties, aided by the introduction of proportional representation (the D'Hondt version). In the 1965 and 1969 elections, however, the Justice Party (JP), having established itself as the main heir to the DP, was able to gain comfortable parliamentary majorities even though the number of parties represented in parliament kept rising. The 1973 elections that followed the 1971 military intervention again produced a fragmented parliament, as did the 1977 elections. No party had a majority in either parliament, but the two major parties (the RPP and the JP) were clearly stronger than the others; their combined percentage of votes was 63.1 in 1973 and 78.8 in 1977. Because of the D'Hondt version of proportional representation, which favors larger parties, these figures corresponded to a total of 74.2 percent of seats in 1973 and 89.3 percent in 1977 (Table 4.1).

The main characteristics (or maladies) of the Turkish party system in the 1970s have been described as volatility, fragmentation, and ideological polarization.[2] Volatility meant sudden and significant changes in party votes from one election to the next. Fragmentation was observed in the increasing number of parties represented in parliament; the fragmentation of seats in the National Assembly as measured by Douglas Rae's index of fractionalization was 0.70 in 1961, 0.63 in 1965, 0.59 in 1969, 0.70 in 1973, and 0.60 in 1977.[3] Although this fragmentation was not too high and the format of the party system was closer to limited or moderate multipartism, the growth of the two highly ideological

Table 4.1   Percentage of Votes and Seats in Turkish Parliamentary Elections (1950–1977)[a]

Party	1950	1954	1957	1961	1965	1969	1973	1977
DP-JP	53.3	56.6	47.7	34.8	52.9	46.5	29.8	36.9
	(83.8)	(93.0)	(69.5)	(35.1)	(53.3)	(56.9)	(33.1)	(42.0)
RPP	39.8	34.8	40.8	36.7	28.7	27.4	33.3	41.4
	(14.2)	(5.7)	(29.2)	(38.4)	(29.8)	(31.8)	(41.1)	(47.3)
NP	3.0	4.7	7.2	14.0	6.3	3.2	1.0	—
	(0.2)	(0.9)	(0.7)	(12.0)	(6.9)	(1.3)	(0.0)	—
FP	—	—	3.8	—	—	—	—	—
	—	—	(0.7)	—	—	—	—	—
NTP	—	—	—	13.7	3.7	2.2	—	—
	—	—	—	(14.4)	(4.2)	(1.3)	—	—
TLP	—	—	—	—	3.0	2.7	—	0.1
	—	—	—	—	(3.3)	(0.4)	—	(0.0)
NAP	—	—	—	—	2.2	3.0	3.4	6.4
	—	—	—	—	(2.4)	(0.2)	(0.7)	(3.6)
UP	—	—	—	—	—	2.8	1.1	0.4
	—	—	—	—	—	(1.8)	(0.2)	(0.0)
RPP	—	—	—	—	—	6.6	5.3	1.9
	—	—	—	—	—	(3.3)	(2.9)	(0.7)
DP	—	—	—	—	—	—	11.9	1.9
	—	—	—	—	—	—	(10.0)	(0.2)
NSP	—	—	—	—	—	—	11.8	8.6
	—	—	—	—	—	—	(10.7)	(5.3)

Source: Official results of elections, State Institute of Statistics.

Note: a. The first row of figures for each party represents percentages of the popular vote; the second row (in parentheses) presents percentages of seats won.

parties (the National Salvation Party, representing political Islam, and the ultranationalist Nationalist Action Party [NAP]) in the 1970s increased ideological polarization and gave the system some of the properties of extreme or polarized multipartism.[4] Short-lived, ideologically incompatible coalition governments were unable to produce policies and control increasing political violence and terror. The system broke down with the military intervention in September 1980.

The military regime that took over power attempted to overhaul the party system by manipulating the electoral laws. A new electoral law was passed in 1983 that, although maintaining proportional representation in principle, introduced a 10 percent national threshold and high constituency thresholds (ranging from 14.2 percent to 50 percent depending on the size of the constituency) with the hope of eliminating the more ideological minor parties and transforming the party system into a more manage-

able two- or three-party system. The 1983 elections, in which competition was limited to three parties licensed by the ruling military
authorities, produced the expected result. The Motherland Party
(MP) of Turgut Özal won an absolute majority of seats with 45.2
percent of the vote. The MP retained—even increased—its parliamentary majority in the 1987 elections with a smaller percentage
of votes (36.3), aided by changes in the electoral system that
favored larger parties to an even greater extent. By that time, however, signs of refragmentation were already present, as became
clear in the local elections of 1989 and 1994 and in the parliamentary elections held in 1991 and 1995 (Table 4.2).

The present Turkish party system is more fragmented than
ever before. The largest vote-getting party in the December 1995
elections (the Welfare Party [WP], heir to the National Salvation
Party of the 1970s) received only 21.4 percent of the vote.
Fragmentation of Assembly seats as measured by the index of
fractionalization is 0.61 in 1983, 0.51 in 1987, 0.71 in 1991, and 0.77
in 1995. Because of the electoral system, with its high national and
constituency thresholds, the fragmentation of party votes has
been much higher than that of seats (Table 4.3). Furthermore, the
relatively greater weight of the two major parties in the 1960s and
1970s (the center-right JP and the center-left RPP), which gave the
party system some stability, has also disappeared over the years.
Each major tendency is now divided into two parties: the center-

Table 4.2   Percentage of Votes in Turkish Parliamentary and Local Elections
(1983–1995)[a]

Parties	1983 (parlia-mentary)	1984 (local)	1987 (parlia-mentary)	1989 (local)	1991 (parlia-mentary)	1994 (local)	1995 (parlia-mentary)
MP	45.2 (52.9)	41.5	36.3 (64.9)	21.8	24.0 (25.6)	21.0	19.7 (24.0)
PP	30.5 (29.3)	8.8	—	—	—	—	—
NDP	23.3 (17.8)	7.1	—	—	—	—	—
SDPP	—	23.4	24.7 (22.0)	28.7	20.8 (19.6)	13.6	—
TPP	—	13.3	19.1 (13.1)	25.1	27.0 (39.6)	21.4	19.2 (24.5)
WP	—	4.4	7.2 (0.0)	9.8	16.9 (13.8)[b]	19.1	21.4 (28.7)
DLP	—	—	8.5 (0.0)	9.0	10.8 (1.6)	8.8	14.6 (13.8)
NAP	—	—	2.9 (0.0)	4.1	—	8.0	8.2 (0.0)
RPP	—	—	—	—	—	4.6	10.7 (8.9)

Source: Official results of elections, State Institute of Statistics.
Notes: a. The figures in parentheses represent percentages of parliamentary
seats won.
b. In alliance with the NAP and the Reformist Democracy Party.

Table 4.3   Volatility and Fragmentation in the Turkish Party System (1961–1995)

Elections	Volatility[a]	Fragmentation of Votes[b]	Fragmentation of Seats[b]	Disproportionality Index[c]	Effective Number of Parties[d]
1961	—	0.71	0.70	1.0	3.3
1965	24.5	0.63	0.63	0.75	2.6
1969	11.4	0.70	0.59	7.4	2.3
1973	28.4	0.77	0.70	5.6	3.3
1977	18.3	0.68	0.60	5.5	2.5
1983	—	0.66	0.61	4.5	2.5
1987	—	0.75	0.51	15.7	2.0
1991	16.6	0.79	0.71	7.1	3.5
1995	23.0	0.83	0.77	5.8	4.3

Notes: a. Total volatility is the sum of the absolute value of all changes in the percentages of votes cast for each party since the previous election divided by two. The 1961 elections are omitted because the DP was dissolved by the ruling military council (NUC), and two entirely new parties (the JP and the NTP) competed for its votes. Likewise, the 1983 elections are omitted because the military government (NSC) closed down all existing parties; thus, the three parties that competed in this election were new. The 1987 elections are omitted because two of the three parties authorized by the NSC (the PP and the NDP) were relatively artificial parties that soon disappeared after the return to competitive politics. Had these three elections been included, the average volatility score would have been much higher. In calculating the volatility scores, only parties that gained representation in parliament in at least one of the two consecutive elections were taken into account. For the 1991 elections, which the WP contested in an alliance with the NAP and the small Reformist Democracy Party, percentages of votes in the 1989 local elections were taken as a close approximation. Compiled by author.

b. Based on Douglas W. Rae's index of fractionalization; *The Political Consequences of Electoral Laws* (New Haven: Yale University Press, 1967), 56.

c. Based on Arend Lijphart's index of disproportionality, which is "the average vote-seat deviation of the two largest parties in each election"; *Democracies: Patterns of Majoritarian and Consensus Government in Twenty-One Countries* (New Haven: Yale University Press, 1984), 163.

d. Based on Markku Laakso and Rein Taagepera's formula: $P_e = \dfrac{1}{\sum\limits_{i=1}^{n} P_i^2}$;

"Effective Number of Parties: A Measure with Application to West Europe," *Comparative Political Studies* 12 (April 1979): 3–27.

right tendency is represented by the Motherland and True Path (TPP) Parties and the center-left by the Democratic Left (DLP) and Republican People's Parties, with little hope of reunification in the near future.

Table 4.3 also demonstrates a high degree of volatility in the Turkish party system, which suggests an almost continuous process of realignment. Although high volatility scores are to be expected, given the frequency of military interventions that wreaked havoc on the party system (the 1960 intervention banned the DP, and the 1980 intervention closed down all political parties), a decade and a half after the most recent retransition to democracy volatility is still high and is rising. This presents a sharp contrast to southern European (i.e., the Italian, Spanish, Portuguese, and Greek) party systems, where "following a critical election, volatility declined and voting behavior became more stable and predictable."[5] High Turkish volatility stems in part from the destructive effects of military interventions, as mentioned, and in part from the fact that Turkish political parties are not strongly rooted in civil society, as is spelled out later. To the extent that the stabilization of electoral behavior is an element of democratic consolidation, the current trend in Turkey seems to be detracting from consolidation.

Another worrisome change in the party system is the increased weakening of moderate center-right and center-left tendencies. The 1995 elections marked the lowest points ever for both tendencies, which have dominated Turkish politics to this point; the combined vote share of the two center-right parties was 38.9 percent, and that of the two center-left parties was 25.4 percent. These totals represented a sharp decrease over the years and a corresponding rise in votes for noncentrist parties. In addition to 21.4 percent of the vote for the Islamic WP, the ultranationalist NAP received 8.18 percent and the Kurdish nationalist People's Democracy Party (PDP) 4.17 percent of the total vote. Although the NAP and the PDP could not send representatives to parliament because of the 10 percent national threshold, the combined vote of the three extremist parties constituted 33.8 percent—more than one-third—of votes cast.

The increasing salience of religious and ethnic issues represents an overall increase in ideological polarization, especially since such issues are more difficult to resolve and are less amenable to rational bargaining than socioeconomic ones. Increasing polarization is substantiated by recent public opinion research. A survey carried out in 1991 within the framework of world values demonstrated that on a left-right continuum 50 percent of Turkish voters placed themselves at the center, 5 percent at the extreme left, 20 percent at center-left, 18 percent at center-right, and 8 percent at the extreme right. A follow-up survey conducted in 1997 revealed 7 percent at the extreme left, 14 percent at center-left, 35 percent at center, 23 percent at center-right, and 20 percent at the extreme right. These survey findings clearly demonstrate an erosion of the center and the rapid rise of the extreme right.[6]

Thus, all three maladies of the Turkish party system in the 1970s—volatility, fragmentation, and polarization—have reappeared, if anything even more strongly. The pivotal position of the WP makes coalition alternatives limited in number and difficult to accomplish. At present, the only possible winning coalitions are the right-left (the MP, the TPP, and one of the leftist parties), the WP-right (with either the TPP or the MP), and the WP-left (with both leftist parties). The WP-left is the most unlikely because of the leftist parties' strong secularist views. The rise of the WP has undoubtedly increased polarization along the religious dimension, since the party's views on the role of Islam in state and society differentiate it strongly from all other parties.

A fourth malaise in the party system is the organizational weakening of parties and of party identification ties, which seems to be part of the more general problem of *el desenchanto* (disillusionment) typical of many new democracies.[7] The seemingly intractable nature of problems, increased economic difficulties, very high inflation, a huge foreign and domestic public debt, growing inequalities in wealth, a sharp deterioration of social policies, and pervasive political corruption have created deep pessimism and disappointment among voters, many of whom do not vote for parties with any enthusiasm but choose "the least evil" among them.

In this rather bleak picture, the only notable positive changes over the 1970s are the seemingly stronger elite and the mass commitment to democracy. Although all major political parties remained committed to a democratic regime even during the profound crisis in the late 1970s, some significant groups on both the left and the right challenged its legitimacy. The radical left was not represented in parliament, but it had many supporters among students and teachers and in segments of the industrial working class. The radical right *was* represented in parliament—even in the government—by the NAP, whose commitment to liberal democracy was dubious at best. There were indications, in fact, that the NAP was involved in right-wing political violence. Finally, many ordinary citizens, including some civilian politicians, believed it was legitimate for the armed forces to intervene in such a crisis in an effort to end the violence and chaos. In other words, not everyone saw democracy as "the only game in town."

Today, the situation seems to have changed considerably. The collapse of the communist regimes in Eastern Europe and the Soviet Union marginalized the extreme left groups. The NAP underwent a silent transformation whereby it became a more moderate, pro-system nationalist party. Expectations and calls for a military intervention subsided significantly. Despite the disillusionment among many voters, this malaise did not turn into an ideological challenge to the democratic system. Increased valorization of democracy as an end in itself is operative in Turkey, as in many other new democracies.[8] As Guillermo O'Donnell observes in regard to the new South American democracies, "The current prestige of democratic discourses, and conversely, the weakness of openly authoritarian political discourses" are major factors working to the advantage of democratic actors. He is also right in warning, however, that these factors are "subject to withering by the passage of time. . . . The influence of democratic discourses depends . . . in part on their capacity to be translated into concrete meanings for the majority of the population."[9]

ORGANIZATIONAL CHARACTERISTICS OF TURKISH POLITICAL PARTIES

Since the beginning of multiparty politics in the mid-1940s, Turkish political parties have generally been described as cadre or catchall parties with strong clientelistic features. If mass parties are defined as parties based on a carefully maintained membership registration system of card-carrying, dues-paying members, with emphasis on political indoctrination,[10] no major Turkish political party qualifies as a mass party—with the possible exception of the WP, as is spelled out later.[11] Although a 1996 survey showed that 12.1 percent of voters were party members,[12] the irregular nature of party registers and the loose link between parties and members suggest that in Turkey what is meant by party *member* is often little more than a party *supporter.* Many local party organizations, particularly in the relatively less developed regions, remain inactive between elections and do little or nothing to give their members a political education or indoctrination.[13]

Membership participation in party activities—other than voting—was found to be highest in the two strongly nationalistic parties, the NAP and the PDP, and lowest in the two center-right parties, the MP and the TPP. The WP (somewhat surprisingly) and the two center-left parties (the DLP and the RPP) were between these two extremes.[14]

The loose link between the party and party members also implies that membership dues are paid irregularly and therefore do not constitute a significant portion of party income. Instead, parties have been financed by state subsidies since the 1971 constitutional amendment, which provides for state subsidies to parties that obtained more than 7 percent of the votes in the most recent general parliamentary election in proportion to the number of votes received. Private donations are also an important source of income for parties.

These organizational characteristics can be explained by the circumstances in which Turkey made the transition to multiparty politics in the mid-1940s. The opposition DP successfully used the long-standing center-periphery cleavage by appealing to peripheral grievances against the centralist, bureaucratic, single-party RPP rule. Most students of Turkish politics agree that the origins of the Turkish party system lie in a center-periphery conflict, which pitted a nationalist, centralist, laicist, cohesive state elite against "a culturally heterogeneous, complex, and even hostile periphery" with religious and antistatist overtones.[15]

Whether the center-periphery cleavage is still dominant in Turkey is open to debate. In the 1980s and 1990s, no single party emerged to stand for the values and interests of the center or received the kind of electoral support the RPP had received in the past. With the fragmentation of the vote, described earlier, no leading party of the periphery exists, either. As Ersin Kalaycıoglu has stated, "To complicate the picture further, the center is no longer what it used to be: Turkey lacks a coherent and compact elite group occupying the center and defending the collective interests of the center."[16] These circumstances were not conducive to the development of mass parties. The RPP remained what it had been during the single-party period—namely, a party of state elites—and the DP found it more convenient to base its appeal on broad populist, antistatist slogans than to try to anchor itself within a particular social group.

Another factor that shaped the Turkish party system was the factionalism that was prevalent in many rural communities and small towns. This factionalism gave the DP ready vote banks, with one faction supporting the DP and the other the RPP. Factionalism contributed to the rapid rise of the DP, but at the same time it made the party a socially heterogeneous alliance united only in its opposition to the RPP. When the DP came to power in 1950, it built an effective rural machine based on the distribution of patronage and pork-barrel benefits. Thus, the original two-party system was based on vertical rather than horizontal loyalties: "Parties concentrated their efforts in securing the allegiance of faction leaders and local patrons who were then entrusted with the task of mobilizing electoral support. In either case, vertical networks of personal followings proved to be a major base of political loyalties."[17]

Later, with increasing rural-to-urban migration, similar party machines appeared in the larger cities and were used effectively by the DP and its successor, the JP. The prevalence of vertical clientelistic networks and machine-type politics helps to explain the failure of political parties to develop organizations based on horizontal loyalties, such as common class or group interests. In the 1970s and 1980s, the increasing complexity of the society and the growing salience of ideological issues led to the party system fragmentation mentioned earlier, although without changing the essentially clientelistic nature of political parties. Metin Heper, a leading student of Turkish politics, has described the present political system in Turkey as a "party-centered polity," meaning a "party system largely autonomous from social groups" in the absence of a strong bourgeoisie in the historical development of the Ottoman-Turkish state.[18]

This last point is related to the overall weakness of linkages between political parties and other civil society institutions, again with the partial exception of the WP. Excluding the 12.1 percent of voters who are members of political parties and the 9.8 percent affiliated with trade unions, only 6.2 percent of voters are members of all other associations. The overwhelming majority of the latter group are members of public professional organizations in which membership is legally obligatory.[19] All organizational links and all cooperation between political parties and other civil society institutions were explicitly forbidden by the 1982 constitution and other laws prior to the 1995 constitutional amendments. But even when such links were not forbidden, as in the period between 1961 and 1980, they were extremely weak or nonexistent. Because of their organizational characteristics, described earlier, Turkish parties do not establish or maintain close ties with organized interests or specific sectors of society. Rather, they maintain autonomy from social groups, shifting from one potential base of electoral support to another or abandoning the interests of their electoral clientele once elected to office.[20]

Organizationally, all Turkish parties display similar characteristics, since the 1965 and 1983 Political Parties Laws imposed a more or less standard organizational model that consists of party congresses (conventions) and elected executive committees at the national and local (provincial and subprovincial) levels. The smallest organizational unit is the *ilçe* (subprovince); parties are not allowed to organize below that level. Thus, the party *ocak* (branches) that existed in villages and urban neighborhoods prior to 1960 were banned by the military government that ruled in 1960–1961, and the ban was continued under the 1965 and 1983 laws on political parties. The organizational model imposed by these laws seems consistent with democratic principles, since party leaders and executive committees at all levels are elected by appropriate party congresses that, in turn, are supposed to represent the entire body of party members.

Nevertheless, both historically and at present, all parties display strong oligarchical tendencies.[21] All parties are overly centralized, and the central executive committees have the power to dismiss recalcitrant local committees. Changes in the top leadership are rare and are caused only by exceptional circumstances. Bülent Ecevit (the DLP), Necmettin Erbakan (the WP), and Alparslan Türkes (the NAP) have led their parties for more than a quarter century; and Süleyman Demirel remained leader of the JP and the TPP from 1964 to 1993, when he was elected president of the republic.

Perhaps the most important function of political parties is elite recruitment or candidate selection. As E. E. Schattschneider has observed, "The nature of the nominating procedure determines the nature of the party; he who can make the nominations is the owner of the party. This is therefore one of the best points at which to observe the distribution of power within the party."[22]

The current Political Parties Law leaves the candidate selection procedure to party constitutions. If parties choose to hold party primaries in which all registered party members or their elected delegates in that constituency can participate, those primaries are conducted under judicial supervision. This method has rarely been used in recent elections, however, and all parties tend to nominate candidates through their central executive committees—which, in turn, are strongly controlled by party leaders.

Therefore, the candidate selection procedure has turned out to be one of the most centralized and oligarchical methods used in Western democracies.[23] Central control over candidate selection is both a cause and a consequence of the oligarchical tendencies alluded to earlier. In addition, this control allows party leaders to nominate a relatively large number of political novices (usually former prominent bureaucrats) who have no grassroots support and are therefore completely dependent on party leaders. No special procedures exist for socializing party candidates into their respective sets of norms, values, and issue stands—either prior to nomination or after election to office.

Turkish parties have traditionally played an important role in electoral mobilization through local branches, door-to-door canvassing by party activists, and other grassroots activities to get out the vote. In recent elections, however, they have increasingly neglected such old-style organizational work and concentrated on media appeals and image building with the help of professional public relations experts. The abolition in 1993 of the state monopoly over radio and TV broadcasts and the consequent proliferation of private TV and radio networks has been important in this area. TV appeals that necessarily center around party leaders have also contributed to strengthening their authority and to the oligarchical tendencies within parties. Another factor in the organizational decline of political parties has been the slowing of economic growth and reduced state role in the economy. These changes mean that there is a limit to the spoils parties can distribute to their followers, which in the absence of strong ideological motivations is important in sapping their organizational strength.

The WP is the only party that has avoided this decline. The party is the only one that appreciates the importance of classical door-to-door canvassing by hundreds of thousands of highly motivated, devoted, disciplined party workers. Further, such activities are not limited to campaign periods but continue year-round. Interestingly, WP workers include many women activists, but no woman has been nominated for even the most modest elected office.

The organizational decline of parties is also reflected in public attitudes toward them. A 1996 national survey showed that more than half (50.7 percent) of Turkish voters thought no parties were defending the rights of the oppressed; 30.6 percent thought they were doing so. The percentage of those who believed their own party defended the rights of the oppressed was 85.6 for the WP, 88.4 for the DLP, 82.1 for the RPP, and 85.3 for the PDP. The two center-right parties, the TPP and the MP, ranked lowest, with responses of 45.3 and 37.8 percent, respectively.[24] Another survey showed that political parties were among the least trusted public institutions. The 1997 confidence score (computed by subtracting the total for those who had little or no trust in the institutions from the total of those who had much or some trust) was –40 percent for political parties. Interestingly the armed forces ranked first, with a confidence score of 88, followed by the police (44 percent), the courts (43 percent), religious institutions (40 percent), and the public bureaucracy (36 percent). A comparison of the parallel surveys from 1991 and 1997 indicates a marked erosion of trust in political institutions such as the government and parliament.[25]

The role parties play in issue structuration became less prominent in the 1980s and 1990s, following the collapse of the communist regimes and the decline of the socialist ideology in general. Consequently, the left-right division over economic issues has lost its relative importance, since all parties now support—in varying degrees—a free-market economy and private ownership of the means of production. Conversely, the rise of political Islam as represented by the WP meant that issues related to the religious-secular cleavage rose in prominence. Nevertheless the WP, walking a tightrope in a constitutional system in which secularism is strongly safeguarded, has generally refrained from structuring issues in an overtly religious form. Rather, it has intentionally couched its appeal in such vague concepts as the "just order" and "national and moral values." In general, parties have emphasized valence issues, such as clean government and economic prosperity, rather than position issues.[26]

The relatively low salience of issues is both a cause and a reflection of another general characteristic of Turkish parties—personalism. In election campaigns, the trustworthiness and other personal qualities of party leaders loom much larger than the parties' positions on issues. This high degree of personalism is also responsible for the division of the center-right and the center-left into two parties each. The rivalries between Yılmaz and Çiller on the center-right and Ecevit and Baykal on the center-left make a merger highly unlikely in the foreseeable future.

Finally, since the beginnings of multiparty politics, Turkish parties have been characterized by a high degree of party discipline—particularly in parliamentary voting. Deviation from the party line is rare, and if it happens the recalcitrant MP is usually expelled. This appears to be an outcome of the high degree of centralization of authority within parties, particularly the strong position of leaders. The parliamentary system of government has also contributed to great party cohesion, since the fate of the government depends on party unity in parliament. In other words, party discipline and cohesion are necessary in a parliamentary system, whereas their role is much less significant in a presidential one. Thus, parties can normally be expected to produce and maintain relatively stable and efficacious governments, even though party system fragmentation makes coalition politics a necessary and rather difficult game. Such party unity in the parliament is all the more remarkable in view of the fact that most Turkish parties suffer from a marked tendency toward factionalism.[27]

Given the organizational characteristics mentioned earlier, one may question the place of Turkish parties in the overall classification of political parties. A recent study distinguished among four sequential models of parties: elite (cadre), mass, catchall, and cartel parties.[28] Most Turkish parties combine some characteristics of cadre and catchall parties, with some elements of cartel parties. Features approaching the cartel party model include: (1) the principal goal of politics seems to have become politics-as-profession in which party competition takes place on the basis of competing claims to efficient management; (2) party work and campaigning have become capital-intensive; (3) parties have become increasingly dependent on state subsidies and state-regulated channels of communication; (4) as a result, parties have shown a tendency to become part of the state and to act as agents of the state. In the change from a cadre party model to a catchall or cartel party model, Turkish parties have never gone through a mass party phase. To some extent, the WP is an exception to this rule, as is discussed next.

THE RISE OF POLITICAL ISLAM: THE WELFARE PARTY

One of the most important events in Turkish politics since the late 1980s has been the rise of political Islam as represented by the WP. Although the party's origins go back to 1970, its predecessor, the National Salvation Party (NSP), remained a medium-sized party between 1973 and 1980; its national vote share never exceeded 12 percent.[29] After a modest restart in 1984 as the WP, its vote share rose steadily, reaching just over 19 percent in the 1994 local elections and giving the party control over Turkey's two largest cities and many other provincial centers. The 21.4 percent of the vote and 158 parliamentary seats it won in the December 1995 elections represent political Islam's best national showing ever.

Opinions vary as to the nature of the challenge the WP represents. The party combines religious and nonreligious appeals, as seen in its emphasis on industrialization, social justice, honest government, and the restoration of Turkey's former grandeur. It is unclear whether the WP seriously intends to establish an Islamic state based on the *shari'a* (sacred law) or would be satisfied with certain, mostly symbolic Islamic acts in some areas of social life. The creation of an Islamic state is a remote possibility that would require that a two-thirds majority in parliament pass an amendment to the present constitution. The party's statements on these issues are vague and contradictory, lending themselves to more than a single interpretation.

Ambivalence also marks the WP's views toward democracy. The party's 1995 campaign platform called the present Turkish system a "fraud," a "guided democracy," and a "dark-room regime" and announced the WP's intention to establish a "real pluralistic democracy." Apart from promises to enhance freedom of conscience and to make greater use of referenda and popular councils, however, real democracy was never defined. In the party's view, freedom of conscience implies the "right to live according to one's beliefs," a concept bound to create conflicts with Turkey's secular legal system.

The WP has prudently refrained from challenging the basic premises of democracy and has said that elections constitute the only route to political power. One gets the impression, however, that the version of democracy it envisages is more majoritarian than liberal or pluralistic. In a 1996 newspaper interview, Tayyip Erdogan, the mayor of Istanbul and a strong candidate for the party leadership when Erbakan steps down, admitted that democracy is not the goal but is an instrument for the WP.[30] Similarly, Erbakan stated that democracy is an instrument, not the aim; the aim is to establish *saadet nizamı* (order of happiness), apparently referring to the time of Prophet Muhammad, usually called *asr-ı Saadet* (age of happiness) in Islamic writings. Rusen Çakır, a leading Turkish student of the WP, concluded that "the WP is neither pro-*Sharia* [i.e., a system of government based on the principles of Islamic law] nor democrat, because it is both pro-*Sharia* and democrat in its own way."[31] Erbakan and other party leaders have often stated that there are only two groups in Turkey, WP supporters and potential WP supporters—a notion hardly compatible with a truly pluralistic conception of society.

Regarding the economy, the WP proposes an Islamic-inspired "just order" that it conceives as a third way, different from and superior to both capitalism and socialism. Although the party claims the just order is the "true private enterprise regime," its implementation—if it is even possible—would require heavy state control. Many observers agree that Islamists in Turkey have significantly changed in the last few decades. Thus, whereas in the 1970s the NSP appeared to be the party of small Anatolian merchants and businesspeople, the rise of an important Muslim bourgeoisie in the 1980s made the party much more open to the interests of big business. Indeed, "Since the 1980s, the Islamist sector in the economy has expanded, with large-scale holding companies, chain stores, investment houses, banks, and insurance companies. Particularly noteworthy are the joint businesses and investments that Islamist organizations have with international companies based in the Gulf countries."[32] Thus, the WP has moved from statist, protectionist positions to views more in favor of a free-market economy and Turkish integration into the global economy.[33]

Whether the WP should be considered an antisystem party is an open question. Certainly, it takes pride in its claim to be different from all other parties, accusing them of being "mimics" that seek to ape the West and to make Turkey its satellite. The WP denounces the current economic arrangement as a "slave system" based on the International Monetary Fund, interest payments, taxes, corruption, and waste—a system maintained by a repressive guardian state that contravenes the history and beliefs of its own people.

The ideological chasm between the WP and the secular parties appears to be wide, and no one knows whether it can be bridged in time by gradual elite convergence. Behind its radical rhetoric, the WP often shows signs of pragmatism and flexibility. The WP mayors elected in about four hundred cities and towns, including Istanbul and Ankara, in 1994 have generally acted not like wild-eyed radicals but like reasonably honest and efficient managers. Similarly, the WP ministers in the WP-TPP coalition government have vacillated between moderate and responsible positions and highly controversial symbolic acts intended to keep radical Islamists loyal to the party.

An analysis of the attitudes and social characteristics of WP voters also provides clues regarding the ambivalence of party policies and positions. Earlier research indicated that religiosity (as defined by faith, the practice of Islam, and participation in religious rituals) was a major factor in determining the party preferences of Turkish voters. Thus, according to a 1990 survey, low levels of religiosity are associated with the left vote (although the DLP vote does not show a strong correlation with religiosity), and high levels of religiosity are correlated with electoral support for the MP, the TPP, the WP, and the NAP.[34]

More specifically, with regard to the association between political Islam and support for the WP, recent surveys show that the WP combines religious and class appeals. Thus, according to a 1995 survey, 61.3 percent of WP favored *seriat düzeni* (Islamic political order) compared with a minority among the supporters of other parties (31.1 percent in the NAP, 16.1 percent in the MP, 14.9 percent in the TPP, 8.3 percent in the DLP, and 4.6 percent in the RPP). Among WP voters, however, 23.7 percent did not subscribe to an Islamic political order, and 15.0 percent had no opinion. Among all voters, 26.7 percent were in favor of an Islamic political order, 58.1 percent were opposed, and 15.2 percent had no opinion. About half of those in favor saw an Islamic political order as indispensable to their religious beliefs. There are strong correlations between adherence to political Islam and the class position of the respondents; 14.3 percent of the upper and upper middle class, 18.6 percent of the middle class, 22.9 percent of the lower middle class, and 27.9 percent of the lower class favored an Islamic political order.[35]

Similarly, a December 1996 survey demonstrated that 60.6 percent of WP voters favored including some Islamic principles in the constitution. When the voters were asked why they voted for the WP, however, only about half gave ideological reasons, such as the WP's defense of religious values (20.9 percent), its promise of a "just order" (13.4 percent), and its respect for "national and moral values" (12.5 percent). Under a third (29.6 percent) of WP voters stated that they voted for the WP because they believed it was an honest and reliable party, although 79.3 percent felt the WP was the most honest of all the parties. About half of WP voters seemed to follow the party line on most ideological issues. For example, 56 percent believed women's wearing head scarves should be made obligatory or be encouraged by the government, 49 percent favored separate education for men and women, and 45 percent were in favor of segregation in public transportation vehicles. Over half—59.5 percent—of WP voters thought the Organization of Islamic Conference was the international organization that best served Turkey's interests (as opposed to one-fourth for the North Atlantic Treaty Organization, the European Union, and the UN).[36]

These findings suggest that much of the WP's appeal is indeed based on religious grounds. The same findings also demonstrate, however, that between one-third and one-half of WP voters seem to vote for the party for nonideological reasons. The WP vote also correlates with the class variable. The party's call for a just order seems to have appealed to small farmers and low-income groups in the cities, even though the structure of the just order was never explicit. This appeal is particularly strong in an economic environment marked by high inflation, unemployment, urban migration, deteriorating income distribution, and widespread corruption. Thus, a substantial number of WP voters cited economic problems as Turkey's most important problem overall; among all problems, inflation was mentioned by 8.4 percent, economic growth by 6.9 percent, unemployment by 6.2 percent, and the deterioration of income distribution by 3.2 percent. The largest group of WP voters (27.2 percent), however, saw "anarchy and terror" as Turkey's most important problem. Among the most urgent economic problems, unemployment came first (43.2 percent), followed by inflation (33.3 percent). About one-third (33.1 percent) of WP voters saw their party as the party of the poor and oppressed, as opposed to 53.5 percent who believed it appealed to all sectors of the society.[37]

The fact that the WP has strong roots among the urban poor is also demonstrated by the finding that prior to the local elections in 1994, most municipalities in the low-income, recently migrant neighborhoods on the peripheries of large cities were won by the left parties, but those same neighborhoods are now strongholds of the WP. In fact, "WP support in metropolitan areas is overwhelmingly peripheral and provincial, in the sense that it rests on a politically active 'secondary elite,' highly effective in mobilizing the urban, lower-middle and lower-income groups, and Kurds."[38]

The WP is proportionately stronger in rural areas (54.9 percent of WP voters are rural, compared with 45.1 percent urban), and the WP vote correlates negatively with years of schooling. In terms of occupational categories, the WP is higher than the national average among small farmers, blue-collar workers, small traders, and artisans. Similarly, with respect to the class positions of voters, the WP is overrepresented among the lower and lower middle classes and underrepresented among the upper, upper middle, and middle classes.[39]

These findings go a long way toward explaining the vagueness and ambivalence in the WP position on issues. To appeal to the more centrist voters who have no desire to see an Islamic state in Turkey, the WP must moderate its position and move to the center—in the process becoming a party much like the Christian Democrats in Europe. Some observers believe such a move has already taken place. The WP, however, feels the need to maintain its support among radical Islamists and to emphasize its differences from other parties along a religious-secular dimension. Such a strategy would polarize the conflict and could possibly lead to a breakdown of the democratic system. It is difficult to predict which course of action the WP will take.

Organizationally, the WP is the only Turkish party that comes close to the model of a mass party, or a party of social integration.[40] The Islamists in Turkey constitute the best-organized sector of the society—comprising a large number of associations, foundations, newspapers, periodicals, publishing houses, TV networks, Quran courses, student dormitories, university preparation courses, a pro-WP trade union (HAK-Is), a pro-WP businessperson's association (MÜSIAD), and holding companies, as well as informal groups such as various Sufi orders and other religious communities. Even though most of these groups and organizations have no formal or direct link to the WP, they provide a comprehensive network that effectively encapsulates individual members and creates a distinct political subculture. The WP is perceived by both its members and its opponents as the representative of the Islamist segment of civil society.

The WP, however, seems to lack the intraparty democracy usually associated with mass parties. Membership entails obligations (such as taking part in party work) rather than rights. Party policy is made from the top down by a small group of leaders (Erbakan and his close associates) who have dominated the WP and its predecessors for more than a quarter century, with little input from the rank-and-file membership. Virtually no genuine intraparty debate or competition takes place in the party congresses, which invariably endorse the leadership by acclamation. In parliamentary votes, WP deputies display perfect discipline. The party has effective women's and youth organizations that campaign not only during elections but also year-round. A new member is immediately introduced to party work and is assigned to a women's, youth, or workers' committee or the polling booth committee. In fact, the party's organization is based on polling booth districts, within which each street—sometimes even each apartment building—is assigned to a particular member who, among other things, must get people out to vote on election day. Political education or indoctrination within the party is strongly emphasized and is carried out by party members called "teachers." Each *ilçe* is assigned to a "headmaster," and "inspectors" at the provincial or regional level supervise the political education.[41]

Among its many activities, the WP organization provides some welfare services for its supporters. Reportedly, during one winter the WP mayor of a poor district of Istanbul distributed

1,500 tons of coal and gave out packages of food (250 kilos each) to 3,500 families during the holy month of Ramadan.[42] In fact, providing such welfare services is characteristic not only of the WP but of Islamist organizations in general. Thus, Sencer Ayata, a student of these organizations, has concluded:

> Following the example of similar movements in other Islamic countries, the Sufi organizations have, in the past few years, tended to concentrate their efforts on welfare services, of which education is one. The economic reformist policies of the 1980s limited government expenditure on social services and on the welfare state in general. This in a country in which these services were only at a rudimentary state and at a time when the rapid rural-urban exodus created widespread poverty in cities. The religious organizations have jumped to organize relief for the poor, medical centers, and hospitals that offer treatment schemes and child-care programs.[43]

In the final analysis, however, the WP's rising electoral fortunes seem to be the result of the failure of the centrist parties to fulfill their promises and to provide greater benefits to voters than those offered by the WP.[44]

THE CENTER-RIGHT

Since the first free multiparty elections in 1950, Turkey has been ruled by the center-right parties except during the periods of military rule and occasional brief spells when their chief rival, the RPP, led coalition governments. The center-right was represented by the DP in the 1950s and the JP in the 1960s and 1970s; the present TPP claims to have descended from the JP. When the DP was closed down by the military government in 1960, three parties competed for its votes in the 1961 elections—the Justice Party, the New Turkey Party (NTP), and the Republican Peasant Nation Party (RPNP). As a result, the former DP votes were split among the three parties. The JP eventually established itself as the principal heir to the DP, and in the 1965 elections it won an absolute majority of both the votes and National Assembly seats. Following the 1971 military intervention, the center-right vote was fragmented again among the JP, the Democratic Party (a conservative offshoot of the JP, different from the DP), and the Islamist National Salvation Party. Consequently, in the 1973 elections the share of the JP vote fell to 29 percent, and the Democratic Party and the NSP each gained about 12 percent. Most Democratic Party leaders and voters returned to the fold in the 1977 elections. The NSP persisted, however, as the representative of a distinct segment of voters. Thus, toward the end of the 1970s, the Turkish party system had an essentially four-party format: the center-right JP, the center-left RPP, the Islamist NSP, and the ultra-nationalist NAP.[45]

The military regime (the National Security Council) that ruled Turkey between 1980 and 1983 outlawed all existing parties and permitted new ones to be established just prior to the November 1983 elections. This was a carefully controlled process that led to a limited-choice election in which only three parties approved or licensed by the military were allowed to compete. To the surprise of many, the Motherland Party, led by Turgut Özal, won the election with 45 percent of the vote and an absolute majority of Assembly seats. The MP also won the 1987 elections with a lower percentage of votes (36.3 percent) but an increased majority of seats as a result of favorable (to it) changes it had introduced into the electoral system. The 1987 elections were held after the military-imposed ban on former political leaders and members of parliament had been removed by popular referendum; consequently, they were contested by the four former political leaders (Ecevit, Demirel, Erbakan, and Türkes) who were heads of their own parties.

The most noteworthy feature of party politics in the 1980s was the predominance of the MP, which gave Turkey eight years of uninterrupted single-party government—the first since 1971. The MP did not claim to have descended from any of the old parties; in fact, Özal proudly asserted that he had brought together all four preexisting political tendencies under the MP roof, although a majority of MP votes seem to have come from former JP supporters. Statistical analysis of party votes in the 1983 elections did not show strong correlations between the MP vote and votes for former parties in previous elections, thereby supporting Özal's argument that the MP was not the continuation of any old party but was a new actor in Turkish politics.[46] In other words, of all the Turkish parties in the 1980s, only "the Motherland Party is based on new societal cleavages and mobilization of a relatively new ideological concept known as the new right."[47] Whereas some scholars view the MP "as an extension of the 1980 coup government," others see it as "the initiator of liberal revolutions, antibureaucratic, pluralist, modern, and able to bring together a coalition including a wide range of ideological groups"—thus, a "genuine catchall party."[48]

In the 1983 elections, the MP fared better in urban areas and in the most highly developed regions. The party appears to have "gained support from the upwardly mobile, entrepreneurially minded, pragmatic, modernist groups that were predominantly urban and living in the developed areas of Turkey. This included considerable support from such occupational groups as the urban self-employed, businessmen and upwardly mobile urban workers."[49] The MP's urban accent continued in subsequent elections, albeit to a more limited degree.

The coalition brought together by the MP did not endure. The erosion of MP support resulted from increasing economic difficulties (particularly high inflation) and competition from the other right parties. The WP and the NAP were reactivated, and some former supporters who had voted for the MP in 1983 returned to the fold. But the most dangerous MP competitor was the TPP. With the removal of the ban on political activities of former politicians, Demirel became leader of the TPP in 1987. Under his energetic leadership, the TPP became the leading party on the center-right in the 1989 local and 1991 parliamentary elections, thereby ending MP predominance. The TPP, as the direct heir to the JP, had the advantage of being based in an older, more powerful, closely knit network of local party organizations with strong clientelistic ties; compared with the TPP, the MP was closer to a cadre or caucus party model, with relatively weak local organizations.[50]

Ideologically, compared to the new right, free-market ideology of the MP, the TPP represented a more conservative, populist, egalitarian ideology in the tradition of the DP and the JP. Although both parties tried to appeal to conservative voters through references to nationalist and religious symbols, in the 1980s MP propaganda gave much more prominence to the themes of change and modernization, as was evident in Özal's slogans of "transformation" and "leaping to a new age." In contrast, the TPP engaged in a more populist discourse based on economic justice, egalitarianism, distributive policies, and a paternalistic, protective state.[51] The ideological differences between the two parties have tended to disappear in recent years, however, as the TPP under Tansu Çiller moved closer to Özal's free-market–oriented, antipopulist, antiwelfare policies and the MP under Mesut Yılmaz moved closer to Demirel-style egalitarian populism.

Recent public opinion data demonstrate that the urban-rural factor is still important in differentiating between MP and TPP supporters. In 1996, 54.1 percent of MP supporters, compared with 49.5 percent of TPP supporters, were urban residents. With regard to occupational categories, the TPP was stronger among farmers (35.2 percent as opposed to 29.8 percent for the MP), and the MP was slightly stronger among blue-collar workers, small traders, and artisans. Regarding class positions, the MP fared slightly better among the lower classes, and the TPP performed better with the upper and upper middle classes. Nevertheless, these differences were generally too small to suggest that the two center-right parties are based on clearly distinguishable social bases, leading to the conclusion that the fragmentation of the center-right is less the result of deep-seated sociological differences than of historical events and personality clashes.[52]

THE CENTER-LEFT

The center-left position on the political spectrum is occupied by two parties, the DLP of Bülent Ecevit and the RPP of Deniz Baykal. For a time it was represented by three parties (the DLP, the RPP, and the Social Democratic Populist Party [SDPP]) until the merger of the RPP and the SDPP. Thus, the divisive effects of the 1980 military intervention can also be observed on the center-left. In the 1983 limited-choice elections, the center-left was represented by the Populist Party (PP). The PP was perceived by the military as a loyal and moderate opposition party to the military's choice, the Nationalist Democracy Party (NDP), which was expected to win a parliamentary majority. The National Security Council disallowed the Social Democratic Party (SDP)—founded by a number of former RPP politicians and headed by Erdal Inönü, the son of the former president and RPP leader Ismet

Inönü—which seemed like a more credible heir to the RPP. The PP received 30.5 percent of the vote in the 1983 elections, but it soon merged with the SDP to become the SDPP. In the meantime, Ecevit, who had strong reservations about factional conflicts within the old RPP prior to 1980, formed his own party, the DLP. Ecevit, like all former political leaders, was banned from political activity, so the party was headed by his wife, Rahsan Ecevit, until the ban was removed by the 1987 constitutional referendum.

The ideological differences between the DLP and the SDPP (now the RPP) are not substantial, although they are emphasized much more strongly by the DLP leaders than by RPP leaders. A fairly important difference is that the DLP does not claim to represent the legacy of the old RPP, and elements of continuity are much more marked between the old and the new RPP. Ecevit characterizes the old RPP as too elitist, representing a notion of reform from above—"for the people but against the wishes of the people." Another difference is that whereas the SDPP-RPP program gives a prominent role to the state in the economy, the DLP is more inclined to diversify the economic structure by encouraging cooperatives and producers' unions, with a view to preventing both state and private monopolies.[53] On most other issues, however, the two parties' positions are rather similar. A 1990 survey found that the mean left-right score for SDPP supporters was 3.94 and that for DLP supporters was 4.28, putting the DLP very slightly to the right of the SDPP.[54] Similarly, a 1996 survey demonstrated that differences between the socioeconomic characteristics of DLP and RPP supporters were small. The RPP was stronger among white-collar and upper- and upper-middle-class voters, and the DLP did somewhat better in all other social categories. Although both parties drew disproportionate support from urban areas, the urban character of DLP supporters was stronger than that for the RPP (67.9 percent urban for the DLP compared with 58.0 percent for the RPP).[55]

MINOR PARTIES

The Turkish electoral law does not permit parliamentary representation for parties that receive less than 10 percent of the total national votes cast, and no minor party is currently represented in the National Assembly except for the Grand Unity Party (a religiously oriented conservative offshoot of the NAP), which was allied with the MP in the 1995 elections and presented its candidates on the MP lists. After the elections, seven deputies elected on those lists resigned from the MP and rejoined their old party.

Two other parties that obtained a fairly high percentage of votes but were barred from representation because of the 10 percent threshold were the NAP and the People's Democracy Party (PDP). The origins of the NAP go back to the mid-1960s when the party became an ultranationalist (to its opponents, a fascist) political force led by former colonel Alparslan Türkes, a leading figure in the 1960 military intervention. The NAP played a highly polarizing role during the 1970s in the violent clashes between extreme left-wing and extreme right-wing groups. The party appears to have moved to a more centrist position in the 1980s and particularly in the 1990s, although one can argue whether the NAP moved toward the center or the center moved closer to the NAP's nationalist and statist lines.[56] The NAP, in alliance with the WP, contested the 1991 elections and consequently was able to send some representatives to parliament. In the 1995 elections, the party received 8.2 percent of the vote, just below the national threshold. The NAP still represents an ultranationalist position, especially with regard to the Kurdish issue, but its commitment to democratic processes is more explicit today than it was in the 1970s.[57]

Another fairly important minor party that did not pass the electoral threshold in 1995 is the PDP, representing the Kurdish minority. Both the constitution and the Political Parties Law proscribe ethnic parties, and the two predecessors of the PDP (the People's Labor Party and the Democracy Party) were banned by the Constitutional Court. The PDP contested the December 1995 elections and won slightly more than 4 percent of the national vote. Most of its support came from the southeast, where the Kurdish minority is concentrated; it received more than 40 percent of the vote in two southeastern provinces and more than 20 percent in six others. As long as the relevant articles of the constitution and the Political Parties Law remain unchanged, however, the PDP is likely to share the fate of its predecessors.

CONCLUSION

The historical overview of Turkish political parties and the party system suggests that we observe here a case of deinstitutionalization. Until the end of 1970s, the Turkish party system can be described as an essentially bipolar (if not a two-party) system in which the two highly organized, well-established parties with strong historical and social roots (the RPP and the DP-JP) dominated the political scene. The tendencies toward electoral volatility, party fragmentation, and ideological polarization—which had begun to adversely affect politics in the 1970s—have reappeared even more strongly following an eight-year period (1983–1991) of stable, one-party MP government. These maladies in the party system no doubt constitute an important obstacle to further democratic consolidation.

Along with these tendencies in the party *system,* there appears to be an overall decline in the organizational capabilities of political *parties* (particularly in regard to candidate selection, electoral mobilization, and issue structuration), as well as in the public esteem in which they are held. Although in much of Europe organizational change in parties has generally been from a mass party to a catchall or cartel party model, Turkey seems to have made a direct leap from the cadre party to a catchall or cartel party without having gone through a mass party phase. To some extent, the WP provides an exception to both generalizations; it is the only Turkish party that avoided organizational decline and that approaches the mass party model. As mentioned, public confidence in political parties seems to be at its lowest point ever. Parties are generally perceived as corrupt and highly oligarchical institutions run dictatorially by narrow-minded, uncompromising leaders who are unable to solve the country's pressing problems.

And yet, Turkish politics are still by and large party politics. Most people realize that there is no alternative to political parties in a democracy. Therefore, much of the current debate in Turkey centers around new policies aimed at making parties more democratic and responsive. It is hoped, for example, that the adoption of a single-member, double-ballot majority system will make deputies less dependent on their leaders and more responsive to the voters and reduce party fragmentation by forcing similar-minded parties to forge electoral alliances. Another proposed reform would limit leaders' influence on candidate selection by, for example, making it compulsory for all parties to hold primary elections. Finally, it is hoped that by reducing the state's role in the economy, the spoils of politics will be limited and party work will be based on motives more idealistic than that of personal material gain.

NOTES

1. Frederick W. Frey, *The Turkish Political Elite* (Cambridge: MIT Press, 1965), 301–303. On the importance of party system institutionalization for democratic consolidation, see also Larry Diamond, "Democracy in Latin America: Degrees, Illusions, and Directions for Consolidation," in Tom Farer, ed., *Beyond Sovereignty: Collectively Defending Democracy in the Americas* (Baltimore: Johns Hopkins University Press, 1995), 78–81.

2. Üstün Ergüder and Richard I. Hofferbert, "The 1983 General Elections in Turkey: Continuity or Change in Voting Patterns?" in Metin Heper and Ahmet Evin, eds., *State, Democracy, and Military: Turkey in the 1980s* (Berlin: Walter de Gruyter, 1988), 81–102; Ergun Özbudun, "The Turkish Party System: Institutionalization, Polarization, and Fragmentation," *Middle Eastern Studies* 17 (April 1981): 228–240.

3. Douglas W. Rae, *The Political Consequences of Electoral Laws* (New Haven: Yale University Press, 1967), 56.

4. For this distinction, see Giovanni Sartori, *Parties and Party Systems: A Framework for Analysis* (Cambridge: Cambridge University Press, 1976), 131–145.

5. Leonardo Morlino, "Political Parties and Democratic Consolidation in Southern Europe," in Richard Gunther, P. Nikiforos Diamandouros, and Hans-Jürgen Puhle, eds., *The Politics of Democratic Consolidation: Southern Europe in Comparative Perspective* (Baltimore: Johns Hopkins University Press, 1995), 321.

6. Yılmaz Esmer, "Dini Degerler Yükseliste" (Religious Values on the Rise), *Milliyet* (Istanbul daily), 9 April 1997.

7. Samuel P. Huntington, *The Third Wave: Democratization in the Late Twentieth Century* (Norman: University of Oklahoma Press, 1991), 255–258.

8. Diamond, "Democracy in Latin America," 77; Juan Linz and Alfred Stepan, "Political Crafting of Democratic Consolidation or Destruction: European and South American Comparisons," in Robert A. Pastor, ed., *Democracy in the Americas: Stopping the Pendulum* (New York: Holmes and Meier, 1989), 47.

9. Guillermo O'Donnell, "Transitions, Continuities, and Paradoxes," in Scott Mainwaring, Guillermo O'Donnell, and J. Samuel Valenzuela, eds., *Issues in Democratic Consolidation: The New South American Democracies in Comparative Perspective* (Notre Dame: University of Notre Dame Press, 1992), 21; see also Scott Mainwaring, "Transitions

to Democracy and Democratic Consolidation: Theoretical and Comparative Issues," 311.

10. Maurice Duverger, *Political Parties: Their Organization and Activity in the Modern State* (London: Methuen, 1959), 61–79.

11. Arsev Bektas, *Demokratiklesme Sürecinde Liderler Oligarsisi, CHP ve AP (1961–1980)* (Leadership Oligarchy in the Process of Democratization) (Istanbul: Baglam, 1993), 39–52, 133–137; Sabri Sayarı, "Aspects of Party Organization in Turkey," *Middle East Journal* 30 (spring 1976): 188–189.

12. TÜSES (Türkiye Sosyal Ekonomik Siyasal Arastirmalar Vakfi [Social, Economic, Political Research Foundation of Turkey]) Veri Arastırma A.S., *Türkiye'de Siyasî Parti Seçmenlerinin Nitelikleri, Kimlikleri ve Egilimleri* (Characteristics, Identities, and Tendencies of Party Voters in Turkey) (Ankara: TÜSES, 1996) (hereafter TÜSES), 95.

13. Sayarı, "Aspects of Party Organization in Turkey," 197–199.

14. TÜSES, 132–133.

15. Ersin Kalaycıoglu, "Elections and Party Preferences in Turkey: Changes and Continuities in the 1990s," *Comparative Political Studies* 27 (October 1994): 403; see also Serif Mardin, "Center-Periphery Relations: A Key to Turkish Politics," *Deadalus* (winter 1972): 169–190; Metin Heper, *The State Tradition in Turkey* (Walkington: Eothen, 1985); Ergun Özbudun, *Social Change and Political Participation in Turkey* (Princeton: Princeton University Press, 1976), chapter 2.

16. Kalaycıoglu, "Elections and Party Preferences in Turkey," 407.

17. Sabri Sayarı, "Some Notes on the Beginnings of Mass Political Participation in Turkey," in Engin D. Akarlı with Gabriel Ben-Dor, eds., *Political Participation in Turkey: Historical Background and Present Problems* (Istanbul: Bogaziçi University Publications, 1975), 125, also 123–125; see also Paul Stirling, *Turkish Village* (New York: Wiley, 1965), 281–282.

18. Heper, *State Tradition,* 100–101.

19. TÜSES, 93–94. These figures do not include informal groups such as religious communities and Sufi orders.

20. A typical example is the frank admission by Abdullah Gül, a minister of state and a leading figure in the WP, that "what counts is our performance in the government, not what the voters were told" (*Milliyet* [daily], 20 February 1997).

21. Bektas, *Demokratiklesme Sürecinde Liderler Oligarsisi.*

22. E. E. Schattschneider, *Party Government* (New York: Holt, Rinehart, and Winston, 1942), 64.

23. For comparisons, see Michael Gallagher, "Conclusion," in Michael Gallagher and Michael Marsh, eds., *Candidate Selection in Comparative Perspective: The Secret Garden of Politics* (London: Sage, 1988), 236–245.

24. TÜSES, 121–122, 127–128.

25. Yılmaz Esmer, "Birbirimize Güvenmiyoruz" (We Don't Trust Each Other), *Milliyet* (daily), 8 April 1997; see also TÜSIAD, *Türk Toplumunun Degerleri* (Values of Turkish Society) (Istanbul: TÜSIAD, 1991), 22–23.

26. For the distinction between valence issues and position issues, see William Schneider, "Electoral Behavior and Political Development" (mimeo., Harvard University, Center for International Affairs, 1972).

Valence issues "are characterized by only *one* body of opinion on values or goals—they define a condition or a situation which is highly valued by the electorate, and political leaders do not take one side or the other. Valence issues are exemplified by peace and prosperity."

27. Huri Türsan, "Pernicious Party Factionalism as a Constant of Transitions to Democracy in Turkey," *Democratization* 2 (spring 1995): 169–184.

28. Richard S. Katz and Peter Mair, "Changing Models of Party Organization and Party Democracy: The Emergence of the Cartel Party," *Party Politics* 1 (January 1995): 5–28; for a slightly modified version of this scheme, see Klaus Von Beyme, "Party Leadership and Change in Party Systems: Towards a Postmodern Party State," *Government and Opposition* 31 (spring 1996): 135–159.

29. On the NSP period, see Binnaz Toprak, *Islam and Political Development in Turkey* (Leiden: E. J. Brill, 1981); Jacob M. Landau, "The National Salvation Party in Turkey," *Asian and African Studies* 11, No. 1 (1976): 1–57; Ergun Özbudun, "Islam and Politics in Modern Turkey: The Case of the National Salvation Party," in Barbara Freyer Stowasser, ed., *The Islamic Impulse* (London: Croom Helm, 1987), 142–156; Ali Yasar Sarıbay, *Türkiye'de Modernlesme, Din ve Parti Politikası: MSP Örnek Olayı* (Modernization, Religion, and Party Politics in Turkey: A Case Study of the NSP) (Istanbul: Alan, 1985).

30. *Milliyet* (daily), 14 July 1996.

31. Rusen Çakır, *Ne Seriat, Ne Demokrasi: Refah Partisini Anlamak* (Neither the *Sharia* nor Democracy: Understanding the Welfare Party) (Istanbul: Metis, 1994), 128–129.

32. Sencer Ayata, "Patronage, Party, and State: The Politicization of Islam in Turkey," *Middle East Journal* 50 (winter 1996): 51.

33. Serdar Sen, *Refah Partisinin Teori ve Pratigi* (Theory and Practice of the Welfare Party) (Istanbul: Sarmal, 1995).

34. Kalaycıoglu, "Elections and Party Preferences in Turkey," 420–421.

35. TÜSES, 67–76, 118–119.

36. PIAR (Piyasa Arastirmalari Merkezi [Market Research Corporation]), "Siyasal Islamın Ayak Sesleri" (Footsteps of Political Islam), unpublished report (1997), 4, 14, 16, 19, 31.

37. Ibid., 9, 12, 21.

38. Ayata, "Patronage, Party, and State," 54.

39. TÜSES, 106–116.

40. For parties of social integration, see Sigmund Neumann, "Toward a Comparative Study of Political Parties," in Sigmund Neumann, ed., *Modern Political Parties: Approaches to Comparative Politics* (Chicago: University of Chicago Press, 1956), 404–405.

41. Çakır, *Ne Seriat, Ne Demokrasi,* 51–52, 71–73; see also Sen, *Refah Partisinin Teorive Pratigi* 79–101; Ayata, "Patronage, Party, and State," 52.

42. Çakır, *Ne Seriat, Ne Demokrasi,* 185.

43. Ayata, "Patronage, Party, and State," 50–51.

44. Morton Abramowitz, quoted in Ilkay Sunar, "State, Society, and Democracy in Turkey," in Wojtech Mastny and R. Craig Nation, eds., *Turkey Between East and West: New Challenges for a Rising Regional Power* (Boulder: Westview Press, 1996), 151.

45. On the dynamics of the party system in the late 1970s, see Özbudun, "The Turkish Party System," 228–240; on the RPP during the 1945–1980 period, see Frank Tachau, "The Republican People's Party, 1945–1980," in Metin Heper and Jacob M. Landau, eds., *Political Parties and Democracy in Turkey* (London: I. B. Tauris, 1991), 99–118; for the JP, see Avner Levi, "The Justice Party, 1961–1980," in Heper and Landau, eds., *Political Parties and Democracy in Turkey* (London: I. B. Tauris, 1991), 134–151.

46. Ergüder and Hofferbert, "The 1983 General Elections in Turkey," 81, 102; also Üstün Ergüder, "The Motherland Party, 1983–1989," in Metin Heper and Jacob M. Landau, eds., *Political Parties and Democracy in Turkey* (London: I. B. Tauris, 1991), 152–169.

47. Ayse Ayata, "Ideology, Social Bases, and Organizational Structure of the Post-1980 Political Parties," in Atila Eralp, Muharrem Tünay, and Birol Yesilada, eds., *The Political and Socioeconomic Transformation of Turkey* (Westport, Conn.: Praeger, 1993), 32.

48. Ibid., 33, 37.

49. Ibid., 35.

50. Ibid., 38, 40. Feride Acar reports that as of October 1988, about 70 percent of local heads of the TPP were former JP members; "The True Path Party, 1983–1989," in Metin Heper and Jacob M. Landau, eds., *Political Parties and Democracy in Turkey* (London: I. B. Tauris, 1991), 190.

51. Acar, "The True Path Party," 193–197; Ümit Cizre Sakallıoglu, "Liberalism, Democracy, and the Turkish Centre-Right: The Identity Crisis of the True Path Party," *Middle Eastern Studies* 32 (April 1996): 142–161.

52. TÜSES, 107, 113, 115.

53. Andrew Mango, "The Social Democratic Populist Party, 1983–1989," in Metin Heper and Jacob M. Landau, eds., *Political Parties and Democracy in Turkey* (London: I. B. Tauris, 1991), 170–187; Sahin Alpay and Seyfettin Gürsel, *DSP-SHP: Nerede Birlesiyorlar, Nerede Ayrılıyorlar?* (DLP-SDPP: Where Do They Agree, Where Do They Differ?) (Istanbul: Afa, 1986).

54. Kalaycıoglu, "Elections and Party Preferences in Turkey," 415; see also Yılmaz Esmer, "Parties and the Electorate: A Comparative Analysis of Voter Profiles of Turkish Political Parties," in Çigdem Balım et al., eds., *Turkey: Political, Social, and Economic Challenges in the 1990s* (Leiden: E. J. Brill, 1995), 84–85.

55. TÜSES, 107, 113, 115.

56. Ayse Kadıoglu, "Samurai Sendromu ve MHP" (The Samurai Syndrome and the NAP), *Yeni Yüzyıl* (Istanbul daily), 12 April 1997.

57. For the NAP, see Jacob M. Landau, "The Nationalist Action Party in Turkey," *Journal of Contemporary History* 17 (1982): 587–606; Mustafa Çalık, *Siyasî Kültür ve Sosyolojinin Bazı Kavramları Açısından MHP Hareketi: Kaynakları ve Gelisimi* (The NAP Movement, Its Sources and Development in Terms of Political Culture and Certain Sociological Concepts) (Ankara: Cedit, 1995).

5

The Military in Politics

No picture of contemporary Turkish politics would be complete without a discussion of the military, which, since its first intervention in 1960, has been one of the most important actors in the country's politics. The military intervened again in 1971 and 1980. Although each intervention lasted only a reasonably short period, on each occasion the military gained important exit guarantees that enhanced its role in the subsequent democratic regime. One of the aims of this chapter is to study the effects of those guarantees in a theoretical and comparative perspective, particularly as they affect the chances for democratic consolidation.

EXIT GUARANTEES

Much has been written in the 1990s on transitions to democracy and, as one particular mode of such transitions, on the transformation of military regimes into democracies through a reform process. The reform mode of transition is characterized by the fact that the transition process is initiated and controlled by the authoritarian power holders.[1] This mode, in contrast to transitions through pacts or rupture, presupposes that the authoritarian government that initiates the democratization process is politically stronger than the opposition and that the soft-liners (moderates) are stronger than the hard-liners in both the government and the opposition camps.

These characteristics of the reform mode imply that the authoritarian power holders are almost always able to determine the conditions for their extrication from government and to obtain certain guarantees of a share of power in the coming democratic political order. Although such guarantees, usually called *exit guarantees*, can be found in transitions from all kinds of authoritarian regimes and not just from military regimes, because of its special institutional characteristics a military regime is usually better able to impose or dictate those guarantees as long as the military-as-institution retains its internal solidarity.[2]

Exit guarantees are often incorporated into the new constitution adopted prior to the first free elections in the hope that constitutional status will enhance their effectiveness and staying power. These guarantees can be grouped under five headings: tutelary powers, reserved domains, manipulation of the electoral process, irreversibility of actions of the military regime, and amnesty or indemnity laws.[3]

Tutelary Powers

One group of exit guarantees aims to create certain tutelary powers for the military over the policies of the freely elected government. As J. Samuel Valenzuela puts it, such powers involve exercising "broad oversight of the government and its policy decisions while claiming to represent vaguely formulated fundamental and enduring interests of the nation-state."[4] Constitutionally speaking, this can be accomplished in a number of ways. One would be to incorporate into the constitution certain substantive values cherished by the military—such as the territorial integrity of the state, national sovereignty, law and order, socialism, social justice, and secularism—in the name of which such tutelary supervision can be exercised.

A typical example is found in the 1976 Portuguese constitution, written by the Constituent Assembly under the strong leftist influence of the Armed Forces Movement. Article 1 of the constitution describes Portugal as "committed to its own transformation into a classless society." Article 2 states that the object of the Portuguese republic is "to ensure the transition to socialism by creating the conditions for democratic exercise of power by the working classes." Even more significant, Article 3 makes the armed forces a partner in the exercise of sovereignty, according to which "the Armed Forces Movement, as guarantor of the democratic conquests and the revolutionary process, shall participate, in alliance with the people, in the exercise of supreme authority in accordance with the Constitution." Similarly, many provisions of the 1982 Turkish constitution, prepared by a military-dominated Constituent Assembly,[5] referred to the territorial and national integrity of the state and to the modernizing reforms of Kemal Atatürk—values highly cherished by the Turkish military.

An even more effective method of introducing tutelary supervision is to create military-dominated formal institutions entrusted with the constitutional duty of preserving such values. The best example is seen in the Portuguese Council of the Revolution, enshrined in the 1976 constitution. Under Article 142 of the constitution, "The Council of the Revolution acts as an advisory body to the President of the Republic, as guarantor of the proper working of democratic institutions, of fulfillment of the Constitution, and of faithfulness to the spirit of the Portuguese Revolution of 25 April 1974 and as a political and legislative organ in military matters." The Council of the Revolution is composed of the president of the republic; the chief and deputy chief, if any, of the General Staff of the armed forces; the chiefs of staff of the three services of the armed forces; the prime minister, if he or she is a member of the armed forces; and fourteen officers—eight from the army, three from the air force, and three from the navy—appointed by their respective services (Article 143).

The Turkish 1961 constitution, enacted following the 1960 military intervention by the Constituent Assembly—one chamber of which was the ruling military council (the National Unity Committee)—created a National Security Council. Under Article 111 of the constitution, the council was composed of ministers to be determined by law, the chief of the General Staff, and representatives of the forces (i.e., the army, navy, and air forces) chaired by the president of the republic. The council had the power to submit its basic views to the Council of Ministers to assist that body in making decisions and ensuring coordination of national security. The article was amended in 1971, following the military intervention on 12 March 1971. Thus, force commanders instead of force "representatives" were made members of the council, thereby enhancing the status of its military members. The language of the paragraph concerning the council's powers was strengthened by substituting *recommends* for *submits* and dropping the words *to assist:* "The National Security Council recommends the required basic views to the Council of Ministers concerning national security and ensuring coordination."

Following the 1980 intervention, the 1982 constitution further enhanced the constitutional status of the National Security Council. Under Article 118 of the constitution, the civilian members were explicitly enumerated rather than leaving their determination to the law. According to the new formulation, the council was composed of the prime minister; the chief of the General Staff; the ministers of national defense, the interior, and foreign affairs; the commanders of the army, navy, and air forces; and the general commander of the Gendarmerie, under the chairmanship of the president of the republic. Thus, numerical equality of military and nonmilitary members was assured. The paragraph concerning the powers of the council was strengthened as follows:

> The National Security Council shall submit to the Council of Ministers its views on taking decisions and ensuring necessary coordination with regard to the formulation, determination, and implementation of the national security policy of the State. The Council of Ministers shall give priority consideration to the decisions of the National Security Council concerning the measures it deems necessary for the preservation of the existence and independence of the State, the integrity and indivisibility of the country, and the peace and security of society.[6]

This rather broad and ambiguous notion of national security was extended further by the Law on the National Security Council (Law 2945 dated 9 November 1983), also adopted by the ruling military council. Article 2 of the law defines national security as the protection of the constitutional order of the state, its national existence, and its integrity; of all of its interests in the international field, including political, social, cultural, and economic interests; and of interests derived from international treaties against all external and internal threats.

Such broad definitions of national security testify to a significant change in the concept of military professionalism, observed in Latin America as well as in Turkey. The old professionalism of external security is now combined with a new professionalism of internal security, or a new politicized professionalism, according to which "the military sees itself [as] legitimately concerned not only with *defense* against external and internal threats but also with the active *promotion* of the country's ability to achieve its national objectives."[7] A good example is the military ideology developed by the Brazilian Escola Superior de Guerra (ESG) in the mid-1950s and early 1960s:

> The ESG doctrine strongly emphasized that modern warfare, whether conventional . . . or revolutionary . . . involved the will, unity, and productive capacity of the entire nation. Thus those charged with the formulation and implementation of national security policies could no longer restrict their attention to frontier protection or other conventional uses of the army. National security for the ESG was seen to a great extent as a function of rationally maximizing the output of the economy and minimizing all sources of cleavage and disunity within the country. Consequently great stress was put on the need for strong government and planning.[8]

A third way to grant the military tutelary powers is "through ambiguous constitutional references to the role of the Armed Forces as 'guarantors' of the constitution and the laws. [Such power] can also exist informally as a result, for instance, of military self-definitions as the 'permanent institution' of the state (i.e., as opposed to the 'transient' ones such as governments) that can therefore best interpret and uphold the 'general interests of the nation.'"[9] A good example is Article 90 of the 1980 Chilean constitution, which stipulates that the armed forces should "guarantee the institutional order of the Republic." Evidently, "General Pinochet attributes great significance to this clause. In a speech given on August 23, 1989 . . . he stressed this clause as one of the main innovations of the 1980 Constitution, one that finally recognizes a 'natural function of the Armed Forces and Police,' that is, recognizes 'their political function.'"[10]

Similarly, the Brazilian 1988 Constitution, although it was drafted after the first transition, gave the military a "guarantorship" role. Article 142 of the constitution states that "under the authority of the President of the Republic, the Armed Forces are assigned with the defense of the Fatherland, the guarantee of the constitutional powers and, on the initiative of any one of these powers, of law and order." This clause represents an improvement over the 1967 constitution, which had charged the military with maintaining law and order and guaranteeing the normal functioning of the three constitutional powers. The apparent improvement brought about by the 1988 constitution does not, however, "significantly reduce the autonomy of the armed forces. Indeed, while the military is placed under the authority of the president, other powers are allowed to request its intervention in domestic affairs, giving the military room to lobby and play these powers against each other, enhancing its own bargaining strength."[11]

Although the 1961 and 1982 Turkish constitutions do not entrust the military with such an overall guarantorship role, Article 35 of the Military Internal Service Code gives it the task of "protecting and safeguarding the Turkish motherland and the Turkish Republic as defined by the Constitution." Indeed, in the early 1960s military leaders often invoked this article to legitimate their interventions in politics.

Reserved Domains

Valenzuela has stated, "In contrast to the ambiguous and generalized tutelary power, the reserved domains remove specific areas of governmental authority and substantive policy making from the purview of elected officials."[12] Reserved domains imply a high degree of military autonomy in certain policy areas; an obvious example is defense policy.

> Entrenched within special domains . . . the military claims exclusive sovereignty over the defense sector. . . . Under self-defined rules, the military sets its own guidelines, goals and missions, and reproduces its own values in an internal, secluded socialization process. . . . The state is thus split into separate realms of authority: one supported by democratic-electoral legitimacy, the other by the legitimacy which the military grants itself from its purportedly special ability to express the "unchanging national essence." Civilian democratic governments are therefore kept from exercising effective authority over a large and important segment of the state. . . . From entrenched positions in the state, the military not only resists outside direction and oversight; it also exercises and expands undue influence in nonmilitary spheres.[13]

An extreme example of reserved domains is seen in Article 148 of the 1976 Portuguese constitution, which made the Council of the Revolution the sole competent legislative organ in matters related to the organization, functioning, and discipline of the armed forces. The council was also given the power to approve international treaties and agreements on military matters.

The 1961 Turkish constitution did not specify reserved or autonomous domains for the military, other than creating a National Security Council on which military representatives participated in an advisory capacity in formulating defense and security policies. Furthermore, the chief of the General Staff became responsible to the prime minister rather than the minister of national defense, as had previously been the case, thus enhancing his status. The constitution stated explicitly, however, that the Council of Ministers was responsible for safeguarding national security and preparing the armed forces for war (Article 110).

The 1971 and 1973 constitutional amendments, passed under the de facto influence of the military following the 12 March 1971 military memorandum (chapter 2,c), substantially increased military autonomy within the state apparatus. One such amendment exempted the armed forces from being audited by the Court of Accounts (Article 127). Another created the Supreme Military Administrative Court, charged with judicial review of administrative acts and actions involving military personnel, thus exempting the military from review by the civilian administrative court (the Council of the State) (Article 140). The constitution was also amended to allow military martial law courts to try cases involving crimes committed at most three months prior to the declaration of a state of siege and to continue such trials until the end, and even after termination, of the state of siege (Article 32 and Transitory Article 21). This represented a considerable enlargement of the scope of military courts at the expense of civilian courts and constituted a significant departure from the constitutional rule that held that martial law courts are functional only during periods of emergency.

Finally, State Security Courts were established to deal with crimes against the security of the state. These courts were to be mixed courts composed of civilian and military judges, with the latter appointed by military authorities. Decisions of State

Security Courts remained subject to review by the civilian Supreme Court (High Court of Appeals) (Article 136).

The tendency toward increasing military autonomy was further strengthened by the 1982 constitution. In addition to maintaining acquisitions from the 1971–1973 period, the armed forces were exempted from oversight by the newly created State Supervisory Council (Article 108). No judicial appeals were allowed against decisions of the Supreme Military Council (a body composed of four-star generals and admirals and charged with the important task of making final decisions concerning the promotion and retirement of top military personnel) (Article 125). Under the Law on the State of Siege (Law 1402), as amended in 1980, no judicial appeals could be made before administrative or civil law courts against decisions of martial law commanders; further, their civil law responsibility could not be invoked for personal damages they caused. The same law allowed martial law courts to try cases involving crimes—even those committed outside martial law regions—provided they were connected with a case under trial before a martial law court. Finally, the same law substantially broadened the competence of these courts by including a large number of criminal offenses within their scope.

Manipulation of the Electoral Process

Departing military regimes may attempt to manipulate the electoral process to preserve for themselves a larger share of power in the coming democratic regime. Such attempts may be limited to the first free election preceding the transfer of power, or they may have more enduring effects. They may be done on a de facto basis or be anchored in laws and even in constitutions.

The simplest way to accomplish this aim is to elect the leader of the outgoing military regime president (or some other key officer) in the new democratic regime; well-known examples include General Eanes in Portugal and Generals Gürsel and Evren in Turkey. The election of General Cemal Gürsel, leader of the 1960 coup, as president of the republic by the newly elected Turkish parliament took place under considerable pressure from the armed forces; indeed, his election was one of their conditions for respecting the election results and allowing the parliament to convene. The election of General Kenan Evren, leader of the 1980 coup, as president of the republic in 1982 also took place under highly unusual circumstances. Although the 1982 constitution provided for election of the president by the parliament, Transitional Article 1 provided for the direct popular election of the president before the transfer of power. Furthermore, the presidential election was combined with the constitutional referendum; a "yes" vote for the constitution was considered a vote for the presidency of Evren, the sole candidate.

The 1961 Turkish constitution made all 23 members of the military ruling council (the National Unity Committee) lifetime members of the Senate of the republic (Article 70). In view of the fact that the Senate was composed of 150 elected members and 15 members appointed by the president, the ex officio membership of former revolutionary officers constituted a significant manipulation of the electoral process. Furthermore, Article 68 of the constitution stated that those convicted of crimes enumerated in this article would forfeit their right to be elected to parliament, "even if they are granted amnesty"—a plan designed to permanently exclude former Democratic Party deputies, convicted by the military, from membership. This obstacle was removed by a constitutional amendment in 1974.

The military regime of the period 1980–1983 carried out far more extensive electoral manipulations. Transitional Article 4 of the 1982 constitution introduced bans on political activities of former politicians. Thus, the leaders, deputy leaders, secretaries-general, and members of the executive committees of all four major parties from the pre-1980 period were barred from forming or becoming members of political parties and from being nominated or elected to parliament or local government bodies for a period of ten years. A less severe ban kept former deputies of those parties from forming political parties or becoming members of their central executive bodies for five years but not from being elected to parliament. The bans were repealed by the constitutional referendum on 6 September 1987.

The ruling National Security Council also carefully controlled the parliamentary elections held on 6 November 1983. Only three parties were allowed to compete in the elections, two of which (the Nationalist Democracy Party and the Populist Party) were essentially creations of the military regime. The Grand Turkey Party, organized by some members of the former Justice Party, was directly banned by the council. The TPP and the SDP that sought to capture the votes of the JP and the RPP, respectively, were not allowed to contest the elections. The council also vetoed hundreds of candidates on the lists of even the three licensed parties. In short, the 1983 parliamentary election was no more than a limited-choice election.

Following the elections, the former National Security Council was transformed into a Presidential Council for a period of six years. The council had only advisory powers, although its members enjoyed full parliamentary immunity (Transitional Article 2).

Irreversibility of Actions of the Military Regime

Departing military regimes may attempt to make some of their actions irreversible or at least difficult to reverse. A typical example can again be found in the Portuguese transition. The 1976 constitution banned all constitutional amendments during the first legislative period following the transition (which ended on 14 October 1980). The Assembly of the Republic would then resume its power to amend the constitution, but once it approved an amendment the second legislative period would automatically end (Article 286, paragraph 1). Subsequent amendments could be passed only once every five years unless a four-fifths majority of the full membership of the Assembly decided otherwise (Article 287). The constitution also provided for a long list of immutable principles that could not be changed even by constitutional amendment. Interestingly, those principles included such highly ideological goals as "collectivization of the main means of production and land and of natural resources and the abolition of monopolies and large estates" (Article 290).

Similarly, both Turkish military regimes attempted to make their actions difficult to reverse. Thus, both the 1961 (Transitional Article 4) and 1982 (Transitional Article 15) constitutions provided that laws passed by the ruling military council could not be challenged for unconstitutionality before the Constitutional Court, even after the transition to democracy. Although, like any laws, such laws remained subject to change or repeal by parliament, this restriction on the competence of the Constitutional Court constituted an important roadblock to attempts to clean up the "authoritarian debris," as Brazilians call it.[14] In the Turkish case, the restriction provided by the 1982 constitution was far more consequential because the authoritarian debris left by the National Security Council was much greater than that of its predecessor. Unlike the National Unity Committee in 1960–1961, the council attempted a major restructuring of the Turkish constitutional and legal system, passing more than 600 laws (535 laws and 91 decree-laws) that regulated such vital areas as elections, political parties, the judiciary, the police, martial law and emergency rule, local governments, universities, the Radio and Television Corporation, associations, trade unions, public professional organizations, collective bargaining and strikes, the press, and the right to assembly, among many others.[15]

The Chilean military regime viewed the 1980 constitution— which it dictated—as one of its "most important legacies,"[16] and that was also the view of the Turkish National Security Council regime with regard to the 1982 constitution. General Evren often described himself as the "guarantor" of that constitution. More important, Transitional Article 9 of the 1982 constitution gave the president of the republic extensive veto powers over constitutional amendments. Thus, for a six-year period following the convening of the newly elected parliament, the presidential veto of constitutional amendments could be overridden only by a three-fourths (instead of the usual two-thirds) majority of the full membership of parliament. President Evren, however, did not use this power when parliament amended the constitution in 1987 to allow a referendum on abolishing the ban on political activities of former politicians.

Amnesty Laws

One of the most common exit guarantees for departing military regimes is an amnesty law on crimes, particularly human rights violations, committed by the leaders and officials of the regime.[17] Such laws were passed in Chile, Brazil, and even Uruguay, where civil-military relations are the most compatible with democratic government of any newly democratizing regime in Latin America.[18]

In Turkey, both military regimes incorporated guarantees against judicial investigation and prosecution into the constitution. The 1961 (Transitional Article 4) and 1982 (Transitional Article 15) constitutions protected members of the ruling military councils, members of the government, and all officials acting on their orders against criminal and civil proceedings; no recourse to any court was allowed involving those officials' criminal, financial, or civil responsibilities.

EXIT GUARANTEES AND
DEMOCRATIC CONSOLIDATION

Exit guarantees for departing military regimes can be conceived as facilitating the transition to a democratic regime. But something that facilitated that first transition may be an obstacle to the second transition (i.e., to a consolidated democracy). "Building a consolidated democracy," Valenzuela argues, "very often requires abandoning or altering arrangements, agreements, and institutions that may have facilitated the first transition (by providing guarantees to authoritarian rulers and the forces backing them) but that are inimical to the second."[19] Felipe Agüero concurs that "this *expansive entrenchment* of the military . . . may become a lasting legacy of the previous authoritarian period, and one that could certainly hinder the consolidation of democracy, eventually threatening its very survival."[20]

The removal of these obstacles to democratic consolidation is not impossible in the long or even the medium run. Thus, extensive constitutional revisions in Portugal in 1982 and 1989 eliminated the authoritarian legacy left by the provisional military government of 1974–1976. In Turkey too, important steps were taken to restore a degree of democratic normalcy to civil-military relations, as is spelled out later.

Two important, interrelated factors that affect the long-term fate of exit guarantees are the probability of a military coup or insurrection and the degree of unity or disunity among civilian political forces with regard to the military's role in politics. As Valenzuela correctly argues,

> Democratic consolidation cannot occur if military coups or insurrections are also seen by significant political actors as possible means to substitute governments. This is the basic linchpin underlying all the other elements that detract from the consolidation process, for tutelary powers, reserved domains, and electoral discriminations would be impossible to maintain in the long run were it not for the threat of overthrowing democratical-

ly elected authorities. . . . The democratic method is thereby sub-
verted to a large extent even when regularly scheduled elections
are not interrupted, i.e., when there are no coups or successful
insurrections. This then generates a vicious cycle of perverse
institutionalization.[21]

In this sense, a credible threat of a coup fundamentally alters the
expectations and calculations of civilian political actors, leading
them to act in ways that detract from democratic consolidation—
such as seeking alliances with the military or inviting the military
to intervene.

The second factor is also very important because disunity
among civilian political forces over the proper role of the military
gives the latter a powerful incentive to intervene in politics and to
attempt to maintain or increase its political influence.
Commenting on the recent Latin American experience, Agüero
observes that "by failing to display a united front, civilians have
shown no common understanding of the obstacles which the military present for the prospects of democratic consolidation. A critical deterrent against the military, which would increase the costs
of military domestic assertiveness, is thus given away, opening up
civilian fissures for utilization by the military."[22]

CIVILIANIZATION OF THE REGIME

The 1983 Turkish transition is almost a textbook example of the
degree to which a departing military regime can dictate the conditions of its departure—a feature Turkey shares with such countries as Brazil, Chile, and Portugal. Nearly twenty years after the
transition, however, a significant degree of civilianization seems
to have occurred. Some of the legacies of the military regime have
been removed through constitutional amendment; thus, the ban
on political activities of former politicians was repealed by a 1987
constitutional referendum and was not vetoed by President
Evren. The 1995 constitutional amendments also repealed some
provisions dear to the 1982 military fathers, such as those banning
cooperation between political parties and other civil society institutions such as trade unions, associations, foundations, and professional organizations.

Some other constitutional exit guarantees, foreseen for a six-

year period from the convening of the first freely elected
Assembly, ended automatically in 1989. One such guarantee was
the transformation of the ruling National Security Council (NSC)
(with the exception of Evren, who became president of the republic in 1982) into an advisory Presidential Council. As William Hale
observes, however, "There is no clear evidence that [the council]
played any crucial role in government after 1983. . . . Its main
function seems to have been to serve as a graceful form of retirement for the members of the former junta."[23] Another transitional
guarantee involved strengthened presidential veto power of constitutional amendments. Thus, in the initial six-year period, a
presidential veto of a constitutional amendment could be overridden only by the three-fourths majority of the full membership of
the Assembly instead of the normal two-thirds majority. Finally,
Evren's election as president of the republic for a seven-year period was intended to assure the military of a degree of continuity
with the NSC regime.

In the post-1983 period, however, civilianization was less a
matter of formal constitutional change than one of informal practice and adaptation. The Turgut Özal government that came to
power following the 1983 elections slowly but firmly established
its superiority in policymaking.

Initially, a division of functions seemed to appear between
Evren and Özal, with the former retaining his influence in defense
and foreign arenas and the latter having free rein in economic matters.[24] This division did not last long, however. As time went by,
Evren acted increasingly like a president of a parliamentary republic, and Özal assumed effective leadership of the executive branch.
Indeed, Evren played a vital role in the disengagement process.
Had he taken "an actively interventionist stand, then it is likely
that the process of transition back to a civilian regime would have
been far more stormy, and less complete, than it actually was."[25]

In 1987, Özal bypassed the military's candidate for chief of
the General Staff, General Necdet Öztorun (in the Turkish armed
forces tradition, the commander of the land forces becomes chief
of the General Staff), and appointed his own choice. When
Evren's term as president ended in 1989, Özal announced his can-
didacy and was elected by the Grand National Assembly—the
first president of civilian background since the military ousted
President Celal Bayar in 1960. As president, Özal took an active

(to some of his critics, an unconstitutional) role in formulating foreign and security policies, particularly during the Gulf crisis. His personalistic style of handling the Gulf affair led the chief of the General Staff, Necip Torumtay, to resign. Many observers commented wryly that in the past a chief of staff who strongly disagreed with the government staged a coup or issued a memorandum rather than resign. Hale argues that the Torumtay affair "indicated that the army was gradually accepting the supremacy of the civil power, even within its own field of professional expertise."[26] In 1993, upon Özal's death, another civilian politician, Süleyman Demirel (at that time prime minister and leader of the True Path Party), was elected president. Thus, despite little formal change in institutions, important steps have been taken toward the civilianization of the regime.

The relatively smooth disengagement of the military from politics in the post-1983 period led many observers to think that a satisfactory degree of civilian control over the military had been achieved and that Turkey was no longer fundamentally different from established Western democracies in that respect. Hale argues that "by the beginning of the 1990s it was apparent that the armed forces chiefs were beginning to abandon their traditional position of semi-autonomy within the state structure, in which defense policy was regarded as their private preserve, outside the control of the elected politicians. . . . The Turkish army's political role was now weaker than at any time since the 1950s. . . . There was a gradual shift towards a new balance, in which the generals would become the servants of an elected government, as in the Western democracies."[27] Ahmet Evin argues similarly that "a working relationship between the president [Evren] and the political executive at the top made it easier for the military to withdraw into the barracks. Assured of its continued influence at the highest level, the military gradually relaxed its control over the civilian regime and devolved its powers to the political authority. . . . Civilianization of politics was fully realized in 1989, with the election of the first civilian president since the 1950s."[28] On the basis of their study of the memoirs and public statements of three recent chiefs of the General Staff (Kenan Evren, Necip Torumtay, and Dogan Güres), Metin Heper and Aylin Güney conclude that "as the Third Turkish Republic entered its second decade, civil-military relations came close to the liberal-democratic model."[29]

These conclusions seem prematurely optimistic, however, and the evidence they present is somewhat mixed. For example, Torumtay is quoted by Heper and Güney as saying that "the military (1) should have as much autonomy as possible from the civilian authority; (2) should be consulted on matters that also have military aspects; and (3) should have the last word on solely military issues." Güres believes that "the military in Turkey was not only responsible for defending the country against its external enemies, but also for defending it against its internal enemies and safeguarding the modernistic and secular features of the Turkish republic."[30] The military's behavior during the 1997 crisis suggests that it still sees itself in a guardianship role against threats to its deeply felt values, such as the indivisibility of the state and its secular character.

From the beginning of the Welfare Party–True Path Party (WP-TPP) coalition government (28 June 1996), the military did not view WP participation in government with sympathy. Although the military initially adopted a wait-and-see attitude, it soon became alarmed by certain actions of Prime Minister Erbakan and strongly antisecularist statements by some WP deputies. These events led to a dramatic 28 February 1997 meeting of the National Security Council, at which the commanders strongly criticized the government for its permissiveness toward "reactionary activities." The council also made specific recommendations, including making an eight-year secular education compulsory—leading to the closing of junior-high classes in the Prayer Leader and Preacher High Schools.[31]

Following a period of intense tension and increasing pressure from the military, Erbakan finally resigned on 18 June, with the hope that he would be replaced by Tansu Çiller (leader of the TPP) and that the WP-TPP coalition would thus be maintained. President Demirel, however, entrusted Mesut Yılmaz, leader of the Motherland Party (MP), with the task of forming the new government. In the days that followed, parliamentary support for the WP-TPP coalition dwindled as a score of deputies, mostly from the TPP, resigned from their parties to support the new government. The Yılmaz government was based on a coalition of the MP, the Democratic Left Party of Bülent Ecevit, and the Democratic Turkey Party of Hüsamettin Cindoruk—a small party that had split from the TPP. The government was a minority government dependent on outside support from the leftist Republican People's Party.

The events that followed the 28 February 1997 meeting of the NSC demonstrated the limits of the military's tolerance for civilian leadership. Although the military is unwilling to become involved in daily politics and is reluctant to intervene directly, its threshold for intervention would likely be surpassed if it believed two of its fundamental values—the indivisible integrity of the Turkish state and the secular character of the republic—were in danger. In 1997, both the military and many civilians felt the latter was under threat. On the more positive side, in that crisis the military acted more like a pressure group joined by most leading civil society institutions, such as trade unions and businesspeople's associations. Parliamentary support for the WP-TPP government, however, would probably not have diminished if there had been no credible threat of a coup. This leads me to conclude that as long as a threat to these two fundamental values cherished by the military exists, a critical threshold will remain beyond which the military is likely to intervene. Chapter 6 considers the challenges to these values—namely, the indivisible integrity and secular character of the state.

NOTES

1. On the reform mode of transition in general, see Samuel P. Huntington, *The Third Wave: Democratization in the Late Twentieth Century* (Norman: University of Oklahoma Press, 1991), especially 124–142; Scott Mainwaring and Donald Share, "Transitions Through Transaction: Democratization in Brazil and Spain," in W. A. Selcher, ed., *Political Liberalization in Brazil: Dynamics, Dilemmas, and Future Prospects* (Boulder: Westview Press, 1986), 177–179; Alfred Stepan, "Paths Toward Redemocratization: Theoretical and Comparative Considerations," in Guillermo O'Donnell, Philippe C. Schmitter, and Laurence Whitehead, eds., *Transitions from Authoritarian Rule: Comparative Perspectives* (Baltimore: Johns Hopkins University Press, 1986), 72–78.

2. On the distinction between "military-as-government" and "military-as-institution," see Alfred Stepan, *The Military in Politics: Changing Patterns in Brazil* (Princeton: Princeton University Press, 1974), 253–266.

3. The first three categories are the same as those in J. Samuel Valenzuela, "Democratic Consolidation in Post-Transitional Settings: Notion, Process, and Facilitating Conditions," in Scott Mainwaring, Guillermo O'Donnell, and J. Samuel Valenzuela, eds., *Issues in Democratic Consolidation: The New South American Democracies in Comparative Perspective* (Notre Dame: University of Notre Dame Press, 1992), 62–70.

Somewhat similarly, Huntington depicts five types of exit guarantees: (1) The military may insist that "special provisions be included in constitutions assigning to the military responsibility to provide for law and order and national security." (2) Actions of the military regime may be made irreversible. (3) New government bodies dominated by the military may be created. (4) Top military officers may assume key positions in the new democratic government. (5) The military may attempt "to guarantee the future autonomy of the armed forces, particularly the independence of their personnel and finances, from control by the elected civilian government" (*The Third Wave*, 238–240).

4. Valenzuela, "Democratic Consolidation in Post-Transitional Settings," 62–63.

5. The Constituent Assembly was composed of two chambers. One chamber was the 5-member ruling military council, the National Security Council. The other chamber (the Consultative Assembly) was composed of 160 members, all appointed by the National Security Council.

6. Bülent Tanör, *Iki Anayasa, 1961–1982* (The Two Constitutions, 1961–1982) (Istanbul: Beta, 1986), 54–55, 121–125.

7. Felipe Agüero, "The Military and the Limits to Democratization in South America," in Scott Mainwaring, Guillermo O'Donnell, and J. Samuel Valenzuela, eds., *Issues in Democratic Consolidation: The New South American Democracies in Comparative Perspective* (Notre Dame: University of Notre Dame Press, 1992), 173.

8. Stepan, *The Military in Politics*, 172–187 (quotation is on p. 179).

9. Valenzuela, "Democratic Consolidation in Post-Transitional Settings," 63.

10. Ibid., 97, n. 13.

11. Agüero, "The Military and the Limits to Democratization," 162–163. For the Constituent Assembly debates on this article, see Alfred Stepan, *Rethinking Military Politics: Brazil and the Southern Cone* (Princeton: Princeton University Press, 1988), 112–114.

12. Valenzuela, "Democratic Consolidation in Post-Transitional Settings," 64.

13. Agüero, "The Military and the Limits to Democratization," 155.

14. Ibid., 162.

15. Nurkut Inan and Cüneyt Ozansoy, "Yasama Faaliyeti Açısından 12 Eylül" (12 September in Terms of Legislative Actions), *Yapıt*, No. 14 (1986): 3–43.

16. Valenzuela, "Democratic Consolidation in Post-Transitional Settings," 67.

17. For a brilliant general discussion of the choice between punishing and forgiving, see Huntington, *The Third Wave*, 211–231.

18. Agüero, "The Military and the Limits to Democratization," 156–164.

19. Valenzuela, "Democratic Consolidation in Post-Transitional Settings," 58.

20. Agüero, "The Military and the Limits to Democratization," 155.

21. Valenzuela, "Democratic Consolidation in Post-Transitional Settings," 67–68.

22. Agüero, "The Military and the Limits to Democratization," 177.

23. William Hale, *Turkish Politics and the Military* (London: Routledge, 1994), 290.

24. Ahmet Evin, "Demilitarization and Civilianization of the Regime," in Metin Heper and Ahmet Evin, eds., *Politics in the Third Turkish Republic* (Boulder: Westview Press, 1994), 25–26.

25. Hale, *Turkish Politics and the Military*, 296; also Metin Heper, "The Executive in the Third Turkish Republic, 1982–1989," *Governance* 3 (1990): 299–319.

26. Hale, *Turkish Politics and the Military*, 292.

27. Ibid., 288, 290.

28. Evin, "Demilitarization and Civilianization of the Regime," 40.

29. Metin Heper and Aylin Güney, "The Military and Democracy in the Third Turkish Republic," *Armed Forces and Society* 22 (summer 1996): 636.

30. Quoted in ibid., 627–628, 632.

31. Metin Heper and Aylin Güney-Avcı, "Military and the Consolidation of Democracy: The Recent Turkish Experience" (unpublished paper).

6

The State, Civil Society, and New Challenges to Consolidation

The presence of an active and well-organized civil society is an essential prerequisite for a democratic system. Indeed, some have argued that "a vibrant civil society is probably more essential for consolidating and maintaining democracy than for initiating it." Although many democratic transitions have taken place as a result of a reform or negotiation process controlled from above, "even in such negotiated and controlled transitions, the stimulus for democratization, and particularly the pressure to complete the process, have typically come from the resurrection of civil society."[1]

The development of civil society, in turn, depends on many diverse factors such as the overall level of socioeconomic development, the prevailing class and other cleavages within society, the political culture, the presence or absence of a strong state tradition, and the like. With regard to the last point, countries with a strong state tradition in which the state can shape the society to a large extent, the "dominant pattern of interest group politics . . . would depend upon the particular configuration of the state–civil society relationship that has been established in the past, and which still lingers on." Metin Heper argues further that in Turkey "there is a virtually one-to-one relationship" between the degree of stateness and the pattern of interest group politics.[2]

The Ottoman-Turkish state has been characterized by a strong state tradition,[3] by which I mean a strong and centralized state, reasonably effective by the standards of its day, highly autonomous, and occupying a central and highly valued place in the political culture. Status-oriented rather than market-oriented values were dominant. The relationship between economic and political power was the reverse of its equivalent in Western Europe. Instead of economic power (ownership of the means of production) leading to political power, political power (a high position in the state bureaucracy) provided access to material wealth. The wealth thus accumulated, however, could not be converted into more permanent economic assets because it was liable, in both theory and practice, to confiscation by the state.

The Ottoman state, unlike its Western European counterparts, did not favor the emergence of a powerful merchant class. The much-referred-to "ethnic division of labor" meant that international trade was dominated by non-Muslim minorities, but this economic power could not be converted into a significant political role because of the Islamic nature of the state.

Regarding land ownership as another potential source of economic power, the state retained the theoretical ownership of and, until the decline of central authority, effective control over all cultivable land. The *sipahi* (fief holders) were not a land-based aristocracy but a military service gentry paid by the state with a portion of taxes collected from peasants; their titles could be revoked by the central authority. The rise of a class of local *ayan* (notables) in the eighteenth century, who often combined local social and military power with connections to central government and tax-farming privileges, did not fundamentally alter this state of affairs. The status of the *ayan* cannot be compared with that of the feudal aristocracy in Western Europe because the situation remained essentially de facto and lacked the legal basis and political legitimacy of the aristocracy. Further, the effective centralization drive under Mahmud II (1808–1839) deprived the *ayan* of much of their political influence.

In short, the power of state elites in the Ottoman Empire was not seriously threatened. Neither the mercantile bourgeoisie nor the landowners developed into a class that could effectively control and limit, much less capture, the state. Thus, the fundamental social cleavage in the Ottoman Empire was based on a strictly political criterion. On the one side was the ruling *askeri* (military) class, which "included those to whom the Sultan delegated religious or executive power through an imperial diploma, namely, officers of the court and the army, civil servants, and ulema [Islamic scholars]." On the other side were the *reaya* (ruled), who comprised "all Muslim and non-Muslim subjects who paid taxes but who had no part in the government. It was a fundamental rule of the empire to exclude its subjects from the privileges of the military."[4]

Accompanying the excessive centralization of state authority and its concentration in the hands of state elites was civil society's weakness, caused by the fragility or absence of corporate, autonomous, intermediary social structures that in the West operated independent of the government and played a cushioning role between the state and the individual. In Europe, the church was the foremost of these corporate structures, and it may have provided a model of organization for other corporate structures such as guilds, autonomous cities, and the like. These structures had no parallels in the Islamic Middle East. As a rule, Islamic law does not recognize corporate identities. For all of the theoretical supremacy of the *shari'a*, the religious class has no corporate identity but depends on the state (i.e., secular authority) for its appointments, promotions, and salaries.

Similarly, neither the cities nor the artisan guilds played an autonomous role comparable to that of their counterparts in Western Europe. The *ahi* guilds (artisan organizations with a strong religious coloring), which had played some role in the formative years of the empire, were later deprived of their corporate privileges and put under strict government control.[5]

In short, no autonomous structure stood between the political authority and the community of believers. This does not mean premodern Islamic Middle Eastern society was totally undifferentiated, atomized, or regimented. One can speak of a high degree of pluralism among craft guilds, the clergy, religious brotherhoods, endowments, mutual aid groups, non-Muslim religious organizations, nationalities, sects, tribes, clans, extended families, and the like. The penetrative capabilities of the Ottoman Empire, although fairly high by the standards of the day, were still too limited to allow it to regulate the entire range of social relationships. The strict separation between rulers and ruled and the absence of a representative system, however, did not permit this traditional pluralism to evolve into the pluralistic infrastructure of a modern democratic state. Furthermore, the nineteenth-century drive by the centralized state to reaffirm corporate exclusivity in response to European challenges further weakened traditional pluralism.

This absence of powerful classes that use the state to serve their own interests, combined with the absence or weakness of corporate intermediary bodies, produced a high degree of state autonomy. The state—which was not the captive of any particular social class—could make decisions that changed, eliminated, or created class relationships.

Regarding the cultural dimension of state autonomy, it has often been observed that the state has a salient role in both Ottoman-Turkish political thought and in the perceptions of the people. The state is valued in its own right, is relatively autonomous from society, and plays a tutelary and paternalistic role. This paternalistic image is reflected in the popular expression *devlet baba* (father state). Another popular saying is *Allah Devlete, Millete zeval vermesin* (may God preserve the State and the Nation). Ottoman writings on politics and government are replete with such terms as *Devlet-i Aliye* (sublime State), *hikmet-i hükümet* (raison d'etat), and *Devletin ali menfaatleri* (sublime interests of the State). Such notions readily found their place in the political discourse of the Turkish republic. Indeed, the preamble of the 1982 Turkish constitution described the State (always with a capital S) as *kutsal Türk Devleti* (sacred), adding that no thoughts or opinions could find protection against "Turkish national interests"—presumably meaning state interests as defined by the state apparatus.

The exaltation of the state has been fostered consistently through the educational system and the military. Indeed, the military and (at least until recently) the civilian bureaucracy have traditionally seen themselves as guardians of the state and protectors of public interest. Consequently, they have viewed with suspicion all particularistic interests and the political parties that represent them.[6] Negative attitudes also prevail with regard to most interest groups; in fact, the term *interest group* still has a somewhat pejorative meaning in Turkish. "Throughout the multi-party era," Robert Bianchi argues, "much of the political elite has continued to share a lingering fear that unless partitive interests are repressed, closely regulated, or prudently harmonized, divisions along such lines as class, religion, and region will threaten both the unity of the nation and the authority of the state."[7]

The growth of associational life in Turkey has been impeded by the strong state tradition and the highly centralized government. After a promising start in the Second Constitutionalist period (1908–1918), voluntary associations remained under the strict control of the state during the single-party era.

> Under the influence of the highly restrictive 1938 Law of Associations, adopted in the final year of Kemalist rule, the total number of associations grew slowly from a handful of 205 organizations in 1938 to a modest 820 groups in 1946. Given the explicit prohibition against associations based on social class, associational life in this period consisted mainly of local sporting clubs that were concentrated in the metropolitan centers of Istanbul, Ankara, and Izmir. During the last few years of the one party era, from the liberalizing amendments to the Law of Associations in 1946 until the 1950 elections, the total number of groups grew rapidly to over 2,000. The end of the formal ban on class organizations was followed by a notable increase in occupational associations during this period. . . . The greatest explosion of association formation clearly occurred during the decade of Democratic Party rule, when the number of associations multiplied approximately eight times to exceed 17,000 by 1960. This was a period of rapid growth and extensive geographic diffusion for a wide variety of associations. It signals the emergence of associability as a nationwide phenomenon, extending broadly though still unevenly over several aspects of social and economic life in nearly every region.[8]

The development of associational life received a further boost with the adoption of the liberal 1961 constitution, which recognized the right of association, stating that "everyone possesses the right to establish an association without obtaining prior permission. This right can be limited by law only in order to protect public order and morality." The constitution also gave trade unions the rights to free unionization, to strike, and of collective bargaining. Between 1960 and 1971, the number of associations again multiplied two and a half times: "By 1970 the total number of associations [had] reached an estimated 42,000. Though the vast majority of these were still small and politically insignificant local community organizations, several of the largest occupational associations had become active and influential participants in Turkey's expanding network of interest group politics."[9]

The Turkish associational universe has long been divided between two major legal types of organizations: *dernekler* (private associations) and *kamu kurumu niteligindeki meslek kuruluslarι* (public professional organizations), with trade unions representing a third, sui generis, intermediate type. Each of the two major types corresponds to a particular mode of interest representation—pluralism and corporatism, respectively. According to Philippe C. Schmitter,

> Pluralism can be defined as a system of interest representation in which the constituent units are organized into an unspecified number of multiple, voluntary, competitive, nonhierarchically ordered and self-determined (as to type or scope of interest) categories which are not specially licensed, recognized, subsidized, created or otherwise controlled in leadership selection or interest articulation by the state and which do not exercise a monopoly of representational activity within their respective categories.[10]

Alternatively,

> Corporatism can be defined as a system of interest representation in which the constituent units are organized into a limited number of singular, compulsory, noncompetitive, hierarchically ordered and functionally differentiated categories, recognized or licensed (if not created) by the state and granted a deliberate representational monopoly within their respective categories in exchange for observing certain controls on their selection of leaders and articulation of demands and supports.[11]

Under Turkish law, private associations approximate the pluralist model, whereas public professional organizations approximate the corporatist model. Trade unions, subject to separate legislation since the early 1960s, are closer to the pluralistic model while retaining their own specific characteristics. All three types of organizations were heavily restricted by the illiberal 1982 constitution and supplementing legislation during the National Security Council (NSC) period. A common feature of all three types of interest groups was the constitutional ban on their "political" activities; the makers of the 1982 constitution did not envisage a pluralistic democracy in which trade unions, voluntary associations, and public professional organizations played an open and active role in politics. This theme was clearly expressed by head of state Kenan Evren in speeches propagating the draft constitution prior to the constitutional referendum on 7 November 1982. Evren stated that political activity should be carried out exclusively by political parties:

> The new Constitution lays down a principle valid for all institutions. Each institution, whether a party, a school, or a professional organization, should remain in its own functionally specified area. In other words, a party will function as a party, an association as an association, a foundation as a foundation, and a trade union as a trade union. Political activity is reserved for political parties. No institution which is not organized as a political party may engage in political activity. On the other hand, political parties should not interfere in areas reserved for trade unions, associations, professional organizations, and foundations. Every institution will function within its own framework.[12]

Thus, the 1982 constitution banned all interest groups from pursuing political aims, engaging in political activities, receiving support from or giving support to political parties, and taking joint action with those parties or with each other (Articles 33, 52, 69, 135, 171). These bans were abolished by the constitutional amendment in 1995 (see Chapter 3).

Public professional organizations,[13] some of which date back to the late Ottoman period, were first given constitutional recognition and status in the 1961 constitution (Article 122). The article states that "public professional organizations are established by law; their bodies are elected by themselves from among their own members. Administrative authorities may not remove from office or temporarily suspend their elected bodies without a court decision. The regulations, administration and activities of professional organizations may not be against democratic principles." The 1982 constitution (Article 135) gave a more detailed definition of these organizations:

> Public professional organizations and their unions are public corporate bodies established by law with the objectives of meeting the common needs of the members of a given profession, of facilitating their professional activities, of ensuring the development of the profession in keeping with public interest, of safeguarding professional discipline and ethics in order to ensure integrity and trust in relations among [the profession's] mem-

bers and with the public. Their bodies shall be elected by their own members by secret ballot in accordance with the procedure set forth in law and under judicial supervision.

As a consequence, public professional organizations in Turkey have a hybrid, if not a sui generis, nature. On the one hand, their structuring brings together members of certain professions to promote professional interests; their members do not normally work for the government, and their functions as organizations are essentially nongovernmental; and they elect their own bodies from among their members without interference from government authorities. On the other hand, these organizations are created by law; membership is obligatory in the sense that except for those regularly employed in public corporations, nobody can practice his or her profession without becoming a member of the relevant professional organization; they exercise certain regulatory and disciplinary powers that are derived from public law; as with other decentralized administrative bodies (local governments and public corporations), they are subject to the administrative tutelage and supervision of central administrative authorities; and again like other administrative agencies, their acts and actions are subject to judicial review by administrative courts rather than by general courts. For all of these reasons, there is no doubt that the public character of these organizations predominates and that they are public corporate bodies.

Although constitutional recognition came only in 1961, many public professional organizations have existed for a long time. At present, ten categories of these organizations exist:

1. chambers of commerce and industry, chambers of commerce, chambers of industry, chambers of maritime trade, chambers of trade exchanges, and the Turkish Union of Chambers of Commerce, Industry, Maritime Trade, and Trade Exchange;
2. chambers of agriculture, and the Union of Chambers of Agriculture;
3. associations of small traders and artisans, and their federations and confederations;
4. bar associations, and the Turkish Union of Bar Associations;

5. medical associations, and the Turkish Union of Medical Associations;
6. associations of veterinarians, and the Turkish Union of Veterinary Medicine;
7. associations of dentists, and the Turkish Union of Dentistry;
8. associations of pharmacologists, and the Turkish Union of Pharmacologists;
9. chambers of engineers and architects, and the Turkish Union of the Chambers of Engineers and Architects; and
10. chambers of notary publics, and the Turkish Union of Notary Publics.

In comparing the overall effectiveness of corporatist and pluralist associations, Bianchi has argued:

> The existing institutional structure of Turkish associational life provides a much firmer base for the further expansion of corporatism than for the gradual development of pluralist democracy. The network of corporatist associations is not yet universal in its coverage of occupational categories. In many sectors organizational structure remains quite undifferentiated, membership continues to be a matter of form, and participation is generally sporadic. Nevertheless, in terms of organizational strength, financial soundness, control over rewards to and sanctions against members, and effective access to authoritative decision makers, the corporatist network enjoys a clear superiority over the still sprawling and fragmented pluralist network. In contrast to the fitful, uneven, and highly visible development of voluntary associability, the network of modern Turkish corporatism has expanded slowly, steadily, and quietly.[14]

Business interests are represented by one corporatist-type organization (the Turkish Union of Chambers of Commerce, Industry, Maritime Trade, and Trade Exchange [TOBB]) and a number of private associations. Among the latter, the most prominent is Turkish Industrialists' and Businessmen's Association (TÜSIAD), founded in 1971 by a group of leading industrialists who felt their interests were inadequately served by TOBB. TÜSIAD, although a relatively small association with a select membership (in 1989 it had 473 member companies), "accounts for about half the production and employment of [the] (private) manufacturing industry. Because leading industrialists also own banks, a large proportion of the private sector banking community as well as insurance companies, construction companies and other service sectors are represented." A majority of TÜSIAD member companies are large firms that employ more than one hundred employees; most are located in Istanbul.[15]

Much of TÜSIAD's work consists of disseminating information to shape public opinion. Its views are expressed in its monthly bulletin, *Görüs,* and the English-language version, *Private View,* as well as in research-based reports on the state of the economy, government policies, and other social and political problems. More recently, TÜSIAD has taken an active interest in democratization. Its well-publicized report, "Perspectives on Democratization in Turkey" (1997), received a good deal of attention and gave rise to discussions both within the association and among the general public. TÜSIAD has also sponsored reports on the electoral system, human rights, and the independence of the judiciary.

TÜSIAD normally avoids direct confrontation with governments. Its working philosophy was succinctly expressed by its former president, Sahap Kocatopçu:

> The TÜSIAD, in carrying out its activities, will be close to the governments according to the degree of their loyalty to a free market economy and [a] mixed economy. But this does not entail being close to a [political] party. . . . If we wish the dialogue with the government to continue, TÜSIAD should take up problems instead of discussing them in the open. In other words, it should know to keep its mouth shut. . . . Many persons who are in fierce competition with each other in many fields of business have agreed on a common denominator in TÜSIAD. The points that are agreed upon are: (1) Defending democracy; (2) staying outside the orbit of a political party; (3) giving priority to the country's interests.[16]

A major exception to TÜSIAD's nonconfrontational policy was its all-out campaign against the Ecevit government in 1979, which may have facilitated the government's fall. Indeed, after this incident TÜSIAD came to be known as the "association that topples governments."

In 1990, another major business association was formed by a group of Islamist-leaning businesspeople—the Independent Industrialists' and Businessmen's Association (MÜSIAD). In contrast to TÜSIAD, MÜSIAD is composed mostly of small and

medium-sized enterprises; a large majority of MÜSIAD companies employ fewer than fifty workers and were formed after 1980.
Also, MÜSIAD companies have a more balanced geographic distribution than TÜSIAD companies: "Although Istanbul appears as
the site of the largest number of MÜSIAD companies, a significant
number are also located in central Anatolian cities such as Konya
and Kayseri as well as in the eastern towns of Gaziantep and
Urfa."[17] MÜSIAD appears to defend Islamic ethics in business
and favors a development strategy more along the lines of the
East Asian model than the European one.

The Turkish Confederation of Employers Association (TISK)
is another major business association in Turkey. In recent years,
industrialists' and businessmen's associations (with no organic
link to TÜSIAD) and young businessmen's associations have
become active in many Turkish cities. Thus, along with TOBB,
which approximates the corporatist channel, private business
associations representing the pluralist channel are playing an
increasingly active role in Turkish politics.

One would hypothesize that this role would have been greatly enhanced by the market-oriented reforms of the early 1980s,
but a closer examination shows that this is not necessarily the
case. Indeed, significant market reforms occurred in the early
1980s. The reform process was initiated by the minority government of Süleyman Demirel (1979–1980), was supported and
strengthened by the NSC regime (1980–1983), and was further
expanded by the Motherland Party (MP) governments led by
Turgut Özal (1983–1989). The fundamental aim of the economic
reforms was to transform the Turkish economy from an inward-
looking, import substitution–based system into an export-driven,
market-oriented one much more closely integrated with the world
economy. As such, the reforms included removing price controls,
abolishing import quotas, converting the Turkish currency, and
reducing direct government participation in the economy.
Additionally, "Another striking shift has involved the progressive
withdrawal of the public sector from manufacturing into infrastructural activities such as transport, energy and communica-
tions. Hence, the role of the state as a direct producer of manufac-
tured commodities was increasingly relegated into the
background."[18]

In spite of these reforms, the Turkish case does not seem to conform to the "retreating states and expanding societies" syndrome. First, public investment has continued to be a dominant form of capital accumulation, although it has shifted from manufacturing to infrastructural activities. Second, public banks have continued to dominate the financial system. Third, a number of steps have been taken to strengthen and consolidate executive power, notably that of the prime minister in relation to the bureaucracy. In connection with the last point, we can mention the creation of "extrabudgetary funds" that can be spent without prior parliamentary approval and in the allocation of which the central government, notably the prime minister, exercises considerable discretionary power.

Furthermore, since 1983 new layers of bureaucracy have been established, such as the Mass Housing and Public Participation Fund and the Undersecretariat of Treasury and Foreign Trade, controlled by the prime minister:

> In fact, this trend pointed towards not only a decline in the powers of the legislature vis-à-vis the executive, but also those of the Cabinet itself relative to the office of the Prime Minister. The Prime Minister, surrounded by a limited number of ministers of state, special advisers and a number of high level bureaucrats, became the real locus of economic decision making.[19]

Thus, rather than a retreat of the state, a restructuring of the state and a concentration of governmental powers took place in the 1980s. This pattern of policymaking is reminiscent of "delegative democracies," as is spelled out in Chapter 7.

This concentration of decisionmaking powers in the government means that economic interest groups have little say in shaping policies, which has led Ersin Kalaycıoglu, a leading Turkish scholar, to observe that "the role of commercial interest groups in the economic policy-making process of the government is either minimal or non-existent. The major decisions concerning the economy, and even the structure and status of the TOBB, were made without prior dialogue between the TOBB representatives and the government."[20] Kalaycıoglu quotes two representatives of the Turkish business community to the same effect:

> Since the days of the Ottoman Empire, the Turkish private sector has always been nurtured by the state and obtained its power and nectar from the state. Even today a businessman is under

the command of the bureaucrats in Ankara. . . . Most Turkish businessmen make more money from the decisions of Ankara than they do by production of some items. . . . Regardless of the circumstances, the business community must be on very good terms with the government because they always need the support and protection of the state.[21]

What I have said about the lack of political efficacy of business associations is also true of other major economic interests groups (trade unions, agriculturalists' unions, and unions of small traders and artisans). All interest groups must work within the framework of a strong state tradition and an excessively centralized decisionmaking mechanism that give the articulation of group interests limited legitimacy. Therefore, neither the corporatist nor the pluralist channel of interest representation is fully developed; Heper describes the dominant mode of interest representation as one of "lingering monism."[22]

Another reason for interest groups' low political efficacy is the absence of strong ties between them and political parties. Although parties try to co-opt major corporate interest associations by influencing their leadership, the links often remain weak and tenuous. Parties claim to represent the public interest without reference to specific group interests. Thus, the significant growth of civil society institutions in recent years is not yet reflected in the party system.[23] This fact also explains the high volatility in party votes and the low accountability of parties vis-à-vis civil society. Indeed, electoral volatility and the degree to which parties put down deep roots in civil society seem inversely correlated: "Where parties are deeply rooted in society, most voters support the same party over time and across different kinds of elections. . . . Links between interest groups and parties tend to be tighter."[24] The high volatility scores in recent Turkish elections (see Chapter 4) indicate that this is hardly the case in Turkey.

One of the important components of civil society is what Larry Diamond calls "the ideological marketplace" and the flow of information and ideas: "This includes not only independent mass media but also institutions belonging to the broader field of autonomous cultural and intellectual activity—universities, think tanks, publishing houses, theatres, film production companies, and artistic networks."[25] The Turkish press was an important element of the democratic process, even during Turkey's first difficult try at democracy (1946–1960). The liberal 1961 constitution removed most restrictions on freedom of the press, and since that time Turkey has enjoyed a vigorous, free, independent press. The state monopoly on radio and television broadcasts was abolished by constitutional amendment in 1993, which led to a rapid proliferation of privately owned TV and radio channels at both the national and local levels. The media had rightly been referred to as "the fourth power" in the country.

The growing power of civil society was best manifested in the role civil society organizations played in the so-called 28 February process" (see Chapter 5) that led to the fall of the Erbakan government. Following the 28 February 1997 declaration of the National Security Council, the chairs of the two largest trade union confederations—the Confederation of Turkish Trade Unions (Türk-Is) and the Confederation of Revolutionary Trade Unions (DISK)—and the chair the Turkish Confederation of Small Traders and Artisans (TESK) stated jointly that the secular and modern democratic republic was in danger and gave full support to the NSC resolutions with the expectation that the parliament would find a solution to the crisis.[26] A few days later, TOBB joined the chorus; its chairman, Fuat Miras, said that TOBB would be "the pursuer of the implementation of the NSC resolutions" and that its members would "openly express their uneasiness with the government [in] every platform." He ended by saying that the government must go.[27]

On 21 May, the chairs of Türk-Is, DISK, TOBB, TESK, and TISK issued a joint declaration stating that "democratization has been stopped. The fundamental institutions of democracy are being eroded. The freedom of the press is faced with armed and economic assaults. . . . [The] modern secular republic designed by Atatürk is under threat. The fundamental characteristics of the Turkish Republic are being eroded, reactionary movements are supported, and our country is pushed into darkness. Today [religious] reaction has become a major danger." The declaration ended with a call for a new government to consolidate national unity and bring about solutions to problems.[28] The leaders of this "civil initiative" repeated their call for a new government at a meeting with President Demirel on 16 June 1997.[29] The civil initiative—bringing together the country's two largest trade unions, two largest businesspeople's associations, and the confederation of small traders and artisans—was a momentous event without precedent in the history of Turkish democracy. Yet, it is doubtful whether the initiative would have been able to bring down the government if it had not been backed by credible threat of a military coup.

ELITE SETTLEMENTS AND CONVERGENCE

Recent literature on transitions to and consolidation of democracies has tended to emphasize, perhaps somewhat excessively, the role of political elites. Transitions are seen less as a product of structural factors than as an outcome of negotiations and compromises among rival elite factions, which explains the term *crafting democracies*.[30] A related argument, forcefully expressed by Guillermo O'Donnell and Philippe C. Schmitter, is that periods of transition are often surrounded by a high degree of uncertainty.[31]

Presumably, this uncertainty should become less severe in the consolidation phase. The first free elections marking the transition reveal the balance of political forces in the country and their respective positions. Therefore, the behavior of political actors should be more predictable in the consolidation phase; and social, economic, and cultural factors may carry more impact than elite behavior and political crafting. Still, elite behavior remains important in prospects for consolidation. O'Donnell argues that during the second transition (i.e., the transition to a consolidated democracy), "democratic actors should agree to subordinate their strategies . . . to the imperative of not facilitating a return to authoritarianism. This is the great accord or pact of the second transition. . . . Even more than the fate of the first transition or that of an already consolidated democracy, the fate of the second transition depends on the quality of democratic (professional) politicians."[32] Michael Burton, Richard Gunther, and John Higley argue in the same vein that "elite consensus and unity is the essential precondition for consolidated democracy." In their view, such consensus can be achieved either through "elite settlements" (sudden and deliberate negotiated compromises among warring elite factions "that precede or are coterminous with democratic transitions") or "elite convergences" (a more gradual bridging of ideological gaps through electoral competition).[33]

In Turkey, none of the three democratic transitions (in 1946, 1961, and 1983) involved an elite settlement because all three followed the reform (or transaction) path of transition in which the process was strictly controlled by the authoritarian power holders. One can also question whether significant elite convergence took place in the post-1983 period. In the early 1980s, Özal's Motherland Party seemed to have built a successful coalition on the center-right, bringing together liberals, conservatives, moderate Islamists, and former ultranationalists. Özal often boasted that the MP unified the four main political tendencies that existed in Turkey prior to 1980. If this coalition had continued, it could have created a similar tendency to coalesce on the left; however, the MP coalition started to break down after 1987, mainly because of the intense rivalry between the MP and Demirel's TPP.

Today, both the center-right and the center-left are badly fragmented, as was explained earlier, although ideological differences among the parties are not great. In fact, a rather meaningful convergence occurred between center-right and center-left elites over market-oriented economic policies and the need to privatize the large public sector. The coalition government of the TPP and a center-left party functioned reasonably harmoniously between 1991 and 1995.

Elite consensual unity and cooperation among rival party elites are not the distinguishing marks of Turkish politics. Indeed, the lack of such cooperation was one of the major reasons for the breakdowns of democracy in 1960 and 1980. The post-1983 period has been no exception in this regard, although in the 1990s some limited but important instances of elite convergence have occurred. Particularly noteworthy are the constitutional amendments passed in 1993 and 1995 and the 1994 law on privatization. On all three occasions, the major opposition party—the MP—collaborated with the two government parties. The July 1997 coalition of the two center-right parties (the MP and the Democratic Turkey Party) and Ecevit's leftist Democratic Left Party, with the parliamentary support of the Republican People's Party (RPP), is another sign of elite convergence that augurs well for democratic consolidation. A more meaningful test of elite convergence, however, is the ability of the political system to handle two new challenges— the rise of political Islam and the rise of Kurdish nationalism.

NEW CHALLENGES:
POLITICAL ISLAM AND KURDISH NATIONALISM

In the 1980s and 1990s, Turkish democracy has faced two new challenges: the rise of political Islam, as represented mainly by the Welfare Party (WP; see Chapter 4), and the rise of Kurdish nationalism or at least Kurdish demands for cultural recognition. In a sense, both challenges are derived from civil society, as they threaten the dominant position and ideology of state elites, Atatürkism. Yet, one can debate whether the multitude of associations associated with these challenges are bona fide civil society organizations. As Diamond correctly states, "To the extent that a group seeks to conquer the state or other competitors, or rejects the rule of law and the authority of the democratic state, it is not a component of civil society at all, but it may nevertheless do much damage to democratic aspirations."[34] This is certainly the case for the Kurdistan Workers' party (PKK) and its affiliated organizations, and it may well be the case for many groups close to the WP.

Both challenges—obviously the products of numerous factors—are related in some degree to the cultural effects of globalization, which include the growth of ultranationalist and religious fundamentalist parties, increased demands for recognition of cultural and other differences, and the rise of identity politics as a reaction to the culturally homogenizing effects of globalization. All of these trends are related to the weakening of the nation-state and more particularly to that of the welfare state, which has been under a two-front attack from the universalizing and localizing effects of globalization. As elsewhere, in Turkey the economic processes associated with globalization have created winners and losers (particularly among manual workers). With the decline of the welfare state and the erosion of social rights, Turkish social democratic parties have been unable to protect these groups, and the WP seems to have successfully filled the vacuum left by those parties. Indeed, in many urban constituencies WP gains parallel the losses of the leftist parties.

Globalization, however, is also associated with growing demands for the acceptance of diversity and recognition of local and traditional cultures, including religion:

> The cultural pluralism associated with the post-modern age also implies a radical shift in the direction of political activity away from the traditional left-right divide to issues surrounding individual identity. In retrospect, the process of globalization occurring simultaneously in the economic and cultural spheres has been interacting and producing powerful impulses leading to the rise of identity politics as the primary form of political discourse or conflict in the current historical context. The massive transformations and dislocations in the economic sphere tend to generate profound crises of identity and a parallel search for greater certainty, control and protection on the part of threatened individuals and communities.[35]

The results of the 1995 elections demonstrate the degree to which identity politics has become an important factor in Turkish politics. The three parties representing different identities—the WP, representing the Islamic identity; the Nationalist Action Party, representing the ultranationalist Turkish identity; and the People's Democracy Party (PDP), representing the Kurdish identity—reached a combined total of approximately one-third of the votes. There is also growing identity consciousness among the Alevis (Turkish Shiites) who do not have their own party but play an important role within the RPP.

Although the WP's positions on issues were filled with ambiguities and ambivalences, as described earlier, the rise of the WP was definitely instrumental in shifting the most significant social cleavage in Turkish politics from a left-right to a secular-religious division. Basically, "The WP in government was faced with the impossible task of reconciling the two irreconcilable aspects of its political identity. Its moves towards the center would alienate it from its support base, and its moves towards [the support base] would distance it from the center. The WP did not try to resolve this paradox, on the contrary it perpetrated it. Consequently, the WP in government swung from one side to the other."[36] As the events leading to and following the 28 February 1997 NSC decisions amply demonstrated, no elite convergence on the religious issue is likely to be achieved; indeed, convergence is highly unlikely, given the wide ideological gap between the views of the WP (now the Virtue Party [VP]) and those of other parties on this issue. To increase the role of Islam in public life as the WP proposes, let alone to return to a *shari'a*-based government, would mean a fundamental change in the secular character of the Turkish state. Such a move would be strongly opposed by a wide majority of the public, other mainstream political parties, state institutions, most civil society organizations, and—above all—the armed forces.

In the aftermath of the Constitutional Court ban of the WP on 16 January 1998, the choice facing the successor VP will be as stark as before—namely, moving to the center to become a democratic Islamic party or maintaining its radical rhetoric to please hard-core militants. There is no reason to assume the VP will be more successful than the WP in solving this dilemma. Although VP leaders have been careful initially to create the image of a moderate democratic party, public opinion data cited in Chapter 4 demonstrate that more than half of WP-VP voters favor some measure of Islamization of the public domain. Therefore, following a purely centrist path would be detrimental to party unity and would mean a loss of the distinctiveness on which the party's propaganda has been based.

A second challenge to the consolidation of democracy is the Kurdish issue.[37] Kurds represent the only large linguistic minority in Turkey (an estimated 10 to 15 percent of the population). Although Kurdish speakers constitute a majority in many eastern and southeastern provinces, the majority of Turkey's Kurdish-speaking population lives in the country's western regions—especially the large cities—and is fairly well integrated into Turkish society. Since the late 1970s, a separatist guerrilla movement, the PKK, has emerged in the southeastern region. The PKK, however, seems to have the support of only a minority of Kurdish speakers even in that region. In general, most Kurdish speakers appear to favor a peaceful solution that would leave Turkey's territorial integrity intact.

Until fairly recently, no ethnic-based political party represented the interests of the Kurdish-speaking population. Nevertheless, Kurds have been active in all political parties and been well represented (even overrepresented) in parliament. A Kurdish ethnic group, the People's Labor Party (HEP), formed in the late 1980s. Both the constitution and the Political Parties Law proscribe ethnic parties, and the Constitutional Court denied the HEP legal status. The court made the same ruling regarding the HEP's successor, the Democracy Party, in summer 1994. The latest successor is PDP, which contested the December 1995 elections and won slightly more than 4 percent of the national vote. Most of

PDP's support came from the southeast, where it received more than 40 percent of the vote in two provinces and more than 20 percent in six others. Because of the 10 percent national threshold, however, the party sent no representatives to parliament. As long as the relevant articles of the constitution and the Political Parties Law remain unchanged, PDP is likely to share the fate of its predecessors.

The story of the Kurdish parties illustrates the dilemma Turkey's leaders face. Modest reforms in the 1990s have sought to redress some of the Kurds' legitimate grievances. The restrictions the last military regime had placed on the use of the Kurdish language were removed in 1991. The notorious Article 8 of the Anti-Terror Law, which made separatist propaganda a criminal offense, was modified in 1995. The offense is now more narrowly defined, and jail terms are lighter, but this category of "thought crime" has not been abolished. Yet, to legalize ethnic parties and enter into dialogue with them on the entire panoply of cultural rights and possibly some local autonomy plans would require fundamental revisions of both the constitution and prevailing notions of the nation-state. This seems to be a major stumbling block on the path to a peaceful resolution of the issue.

The ban on ethnically based political parties deprives the Turkish government of the opportunity to negotiate with legitimate and democratic interlocutors. In 1998, the Constitutional Court banned by a 6 to 5 margin a Kurdish political party, the Democratic Mass Party, led by former minister Serafeddin Elçi. The party, although avowedly representing the Kurdish identity, repudiated violence and sought to find a solution to the Kurdish problem through democratic and peaceful means. Regarding a possible compromise, federal and regional schemes should be ruled out because they would run counter to the unitary nature of the Turkish state, although recognition of certain cultural rights on an individual basis is not out of the question. Most Turkish political leaders, however, feel the timing is not right and that the PKK would perceive such a move as a sign of weakness and indecision. If and when terrorist activities subside, Turkish political leaders can be expected to be more forthcoming.

As difficult as such changes would surely prove, a purely military solution to the problem might be even worse. Such a policy would threaten to polarize the situation even further, given the human rights abuses and other hardships military campaigns inevitably inflict on local civilian populations. Human rights violations have already strained Turkey's relations with the West, including the European Union, the Council of Europe, and the United States. Western criticism of Turkey's behavior, in turn, has created an anti-Western backlash that can only help the VP.

In short, the increasing importance of religious and ethnic issues raises a number of difficult constitutional problems that Turkish democracy has not previously confronted, including the question of Islamism versus secularism, claims of the nation-state versus rights of minorities, and centralization versus devolution. Full consolidation of democracy depends on a reasonable degree of consensus on these fundamental issues. Given the fundamental changes such consensus would require in Turkey's constitutional structure, as well as in prevailing notions of a secular and a national state, elite convergence on these issues is highly unlikely in the short and even the medium term.

NOTES

1. Larry Diamond, "Rethinking Civil Society: Toward Democratic Consolidation," *Journal of Democracy* 5 (July 1994): 4, 6.

2. Metin Heper, "The State and Interest Groups with Special Reference to Turkey," in Metin Heper, ed., *Strong State and Economic Interest Groups: The Post-1980 Turkish Experience* (Berlin: Walter de Gruyter, 1991), 6, 8.

3. On this point I draw on Ergun Özbudun, "Continuing Ottoman Legacy and the State Tradition in the Middle East," in L. Carl Brown, ed., *Imperial Legacy: The Ottoman Imprint on the Balkans and the Middle East* (New York: Columbia University Press, 1996), 135–139; see also Metin Heper, *The State Tradition in Turkey* (Walkington: Eothen, 1985).

4. Halil Inalcık, "The Nature of Traditional Society: Turkey," in Robert E. Ward and Dankwart A. Rustow, eds., *Political Modernization in Japan and Turkey* (Princeton: Princeton University Press, 1964), 44.

5. Serif Mardin, "Power, Civil Society and Culture in the Ottoman Empire," *Comparative Studies in Society and History* 11 (June 1969): 265–266.

6. Ergun Özbudun, "State Elites and Democratic Political Culture in Turkey," in Larry Diamond, ed., *Political Culture and Democracy in Developing Countries* (Boulder: Lynne Rienner, 1993), 247–268.

7. Robert Bianchi, *Interest Groups and Political Development in Turkey* (Princeton: Princeton University Press, 1984), 105.

8. Ibid., 155.

9. Ibid., 155–156.

10. Philippe C. Schmitter, "Still the Century of Corporatism?" in

Philippe C. Schmitter and Gerhard Lembruch, eds., *Trends Toward Corporatist Intermediation* (Beverly Hills: Sage, 1979), 15.

11. Ibid., 13.

12. Quoted in Ergun Özbudun, "The Post-1980 Legal Framework for Interest Group Associations," in Metin Heper, ed., *Strong State and Economic Interest Groups: The Post-1980 Turkish Experience* (Berlin: Walter de Gruyter, 1991), 42–43.

13. Here I draw on ibid., 46–47; see also Bianchi, *Interest Groups*, 129–138.

14. Bianchi, *Interest Groups*, 350.

15. Yesim Arat, "Politics and Big Business: Janus-Faced Link to the State," in Metin Heper, ed., *Strong State and Economic Interest Groups: The Post-1980 Turkish Experience* (Berlin: Walter de Gruyter, 1991), 137–138; Ayse Bugra, "Class, Culture, and State: An Analysis of Interest Representation by Two Turkish Business Associations," *International Journal of Middle East Studies* 30 (November 1998): 526–527.

16. Quoted in Yılmaz Esmer, "Manufacturing Industries: Giants with Hesitant Voices," in Metin Heper, ed., *Strong State and Economic Interest Groups: The Post-1980 Turkish Experience* (Berlin: Walter de Gruyter, 1991), 128.

17. Bugra, "Class, Culture, and State," 524, also 529–530.

18. Ziya Önis, "Political Economy of Turkey in the 1980s: Anatomy of Unorthodox Liberalism," in Metin Heper, ed., *Strong State and Economic Interest Groups: The Post-1980 Turkish Experience* (Berlin: Walter de Gruyter, 1991), 29.

19. Ibid., 32–33; see also Metin Heper, "The Executive in the Third Turkish Republic, 1982–1989," *Governance* 3 (1990): 299–319.

20. Ersin Kalaycıoglu, "Commercial Groups: Love-Hate Relationship with the State," in Metin Heper, ed., *Strong State and Economic Interest Groups: The Post-1980 Turkish Experience* (Berlin: Walter de Gruyter, 1991), 83.

21. Ibid., 81–82.

22. Metin Heper, "Interest-Group Politics in Post-1980 Turkey: Lingering Monism," in Metin Heper, ed., *Strong State and Economic Interest Groups: The Post-1980 Turkish Experience* (Berlin: Walter de Gruyter, 1991), 163–176.

23. Aydın Ugur, "Batıda ve Türkiye'de Sivil Toplum: Kavram ve Olgunun Gelisim Serüveni" (Civil Society in the West and in Turkey: The Concept and Adventure of the Development of the Phenomenon), in *75 Yılda Tebaa'dan Yurttasa Dogru* (Istanbul: Tarih Vakfı Yayınları, 1998), 213–226.

24. Scott Mainwaring, "Party Systems in the Third Wave," *Journal of Democracy* 9 (July 1998): 72.

25. Diamond, "Rethinking Civil Society," 6.

26. *Hürriyet* (Istanbul daily), 5 March 1997.

27. Ibid., 1 April 1997.

28. *Radikal* (Istanbul daily), 22 May 1997.

29. *Hürriyet* (Istanbul daily), 17 June 1997.

30. See, for example, Giuseppe Di Palma, *To Craft Democracies: An Essay on Democratic Transitions* (Berkeley: University of California Press, 1990).

31. Guillermo O'Donnell and Philippe C. Schmitter, *Transitions from Authoritarian Rule: Tentative Conclusions About Uncertain Democracies* (Baltimore: Johns Hopkins University Press, 1986), passim.

32. Guillermo O'Donnell, "Transitions, Continuities, and Paradoxes," in Scott Mainwaring, Guillermo O'Donnell, and J. Samuel Valenzuela, eds., *Issues in Democratic Consolidation: The New South American Democracies in Comparative Perspective* (Notre Dame: University of Notre Dame Press, 1992), 22–23.

33. Michael Burton, Richard Gunther, and John Higley, "Elites and Democratic Consolidation in Latin America and Southern Europe: An Overview," in John Higley and Richard Gunther, eds., *Elites and Democratic Consolidation in Latin America and Southern Europe* (Cambridge: Cambridge University Press, 1992), 323–324, 339.

34. Diamond, "Rethinking Civil Society," 11–12.

35. Ziya Önis, "The Political Economy of Islamic Resurgence in Turkey: The Rise of the Welfare Party in Perspective," *Third World Quarterly* 18, No. 4 (1997): 747. On the rise of identity politics, see also Ayse Ayata, "The Emergence of Identity Politics in Turkey," *New Perspectives on Turkey* 17 (fall 1997): 59–73.

36. Menderes Çınar, "Rebuilding the Center: Mission Impossible?" *Private View* 1 (autumn 1997): 74.

37. For a recent comprehensive treatment of the Kurdish issue, see Henri J. Barkey and Graham E. Fuller, *Turkey's Kurdish Question*, Carnegie Commission on Preventing Deadly Conflict (Lanham: Rowman and Littlefield, 1998).

7

Conclusion

What I have said so far indicates that although it is a second-wave and a not a third-wave democracy, Turkey has been unable to fully consolidate its democracy. Even though Turkey has a comparative edge over postcommunist democracies by virtue of its long-established market economy and relatively free and autonomous civil society, its democratic consolidation lags behind not only new southern European democracies (Spain, Portugal, and Greece) but also some third-wave Central European democracies.

One of the main problems facing democratic consolidation in Turkey is the deinstitutionalization of the party system. Turkey, which in the period 1946–1980 had one of the most highly institutionalized party systems of the young democracies, has been going through a process of institutional decay since the mid-1980s. To be sure, "The notion of institutionalization implies nothing teleological, no necessary progression from weaker to greater institutionalization. Party systems can deinstitutionalize, as they have done in Canada, Italy, Peru, and Venezuela during this decade."[1] In Turkey, party system deinstitutionalization is reflected in growing electoral volatility, fragmentation, and polarization, as well as in the declining legitimacy and organizational capability of political parties.

One reason for this institutional decline seems to be the fact that parties are not strongly rooted in society and that their links to the major interest groups are weak, as explained in Chapter 6. This leads to a seemingly paradoxical situation in which the recent growth of civil society is coupled with the deinstitutionalization of the party system. Most observers agree that the development of political parties has lagged behind that of civil society. Political parties have suffered a significant loss of credibility in recent years and at present are held in rather low esteem by the general public. Furthermore, the closed and oligarchic nature of party leadership tends to stymie the effective functioning of both vertical and horizontal mechanisms of accountability, as is spelled out later.

A second set of problems is related to constitutional issues. As I explained in Chapter 3, the exclusionary method by which the 1961 and 1982 constitutions were developed deprived them of much-needed popular legitimacy. Both constitutions, no matter how deep their differences, were on the whole imposed by state elites on a passive civil society, and they reflected the values of the former much more than those of the latter. Since the retransition to democracy in 1983, almost all political parties have criticized the constitution and have come out in principle in favor of making it more democratic and pluralistic. Yet, so far no compromises have been reached except on minor matters. The 1995 constitutional amendments did not live up to popular expectations and remained limited essentially to removing bans on the political activities of civil society institutions, such as trade unions, voluntary associations, and public professional organizations. The limited scope of constitutional change and the legislature's failure to pass other important reform laws attest to the low capacity of the political system to effect elite settlements and convergences (Chapter 6).

The most frequently criticized provisions of the current constitution are those relating to fundamental rights and liberties, to the independence of the judiciary, and to the tutelary powers and reserved domains granted to the military (Chapter 5). The Turkish military enjoys far greater political influence and prestige than is the case in more highly institutionalized democracies.

Interestingly and paradoxically, however, a majority of Turks do not seem to see democracy and such military privileges as incompatible. The military is still perceived as the ultimate guarantor of secular democracy against the fundamentalist Islamist threat. Public opinion polls have consistently shown that the armed forces remain by far the most trusted public institution. A reorganization of civil-military relations along the lines of institutionalized Western democracies seems possible only if and when the Islamist challenge subsides.

The most serious obstacles to democratic consolidation in Turkey are the Islamist and Kurdish nationalist challenges, as explained in Chapter 6. Both groups confront Turkish democracy with problems far graver than any in its history because successful resolution of those challenges through an elite settlement or elite convergence depends on a fundamental redefinition of the Turkish state. The two basic pillars of the Turkish Republic as designed by Kemal Atatürk have been nationalism and secularism; therefore, state elites, the military, the leadership of the major mainstream parties, and most large civil society organizations—as well as a majority of the public—perceive the Islamists and Kurds as threatening the basic characteristics of the Turkish state. The unsolved (and perhaps unsolvable) nature of these problems precludes progress in improving Turkey's human rights record and consolidating its democratic institutions.

With such constraints on consolidating democracy, what is Turkey's place among the third-wave democracies? What are significant similarities and differences, if any, with other such democracies? If similarities exist, do they warrant a new typology of democracies or the conceptualization of such a type?

The type of democracy that best seems to fit the Turkish case is Guillermo O'Donnell's notion of a "delegative democracy," which he believes constitutes a "new species." Delegative democracies "are not consolidated (i.e., institutionalized) democracies, but they may be enduring. In many cases, there is no sign either of any imminent threat of an authoritarian regression or of advances toward representative democracy." In contrast to representative (or institutionalized) democracies, delegative democracies are marked by *personalismo* (a highly personalistic style of leadership). Horizontal accountability (i.e., accountability to other autonomous institutions such as the legislature or the courts) is seen as a "nuisance" and an unnecessary impediment to fulfilling the president's "mission." The president and his or her technocratic advisers make policy by decree (*decretismo*) without consulting parties, the legislature, or relevant interest groups. Precisely for this reason, however, such policies often face heavy resistance and remain unimplemented. Because delegative democracy encourages personalized leadership, it does not favor the development of strong political institutions.[2]

O'Donnell's analysis implies that delegative democracies are typically found in presidential regimes, and indeed there are good theoretical and empirical reasons for associating the two. Normally, a parliamentary system has far more effective horizontal accountability. A prime minister, no matter how popular, cannot ignore the parliament and political parties the way an elected president can.

The Turkish experience with democracy, however, suggests that even a parliamentary regime is not entirely immune to delegative democracy. Turkey's first democracy trial, under Prime Minister Adnan Menderes (1950–1960), was a typical delegative democracy that ended with a military intervention. The period since 1983 has also displayed a strong resemblance to delegative democracy. Turgut Özal (first as prime minister from 1983 to 1989 and then as president between 1989 and 1991) and Tansu Çiller (as prime minister from 1993 to 1995) both showed a penchant for highly personalistic leadership, often bypassing parliament through the use of law-amending executive decrees. Each made key policy decisions alone or with at most a few favorite ministers and technocrats, sometimes without informing the rest of the cabinet.[3] Election campaigns stressed the personal qualities and trustworthiness of individual leaders rather than party programs and policies. Party leaders were presented as "saviors of the country." Their policies in office, however, typically bore scant resemblance to what they had promised while campaigning.

A defining element of delegative democracies is the absence of horizontal accountability to other autonomous state institutions, such as parliament and the courts. In Turkey, strong party discipline often stymies parliamentary accountability. The key explanatory variables here are strong party discipline and the absence of intraparty democracy. With top leaders in control of nominations and patronage, members of parliament are highly dependent and docile. In recent parliamentary elections, in all major parties candidates were nominated by party leaders with at most a few trusted lieutenants. When a party forms a government or takes part in a coalition government, party leaders also control the sources of patronage, which is as prominent in politics in Turkey as it is in Latin America.[4] The Turkish tendency toward *personalismo* also draws strength from the country's political culture and historical traditions.

Regarding the courts, both the 1961 and 1982 constitutions provided tenure and income security for all judges and public prosecutors. All personnel and disciplinary decisions regarding these officials are made by the Supreme Council of Judges and Public Prosecutors, composed primarily of judges nominated by the higher courts and appointed by the president. The Constitutional Court is one of the oldest and strongest in Europe. The court has generally pursued an activist line: of the eighty challenges regarding the constitutionality of laws it heard between 1990 and 1995, sixty-nine were rendered unconstitutional. Yet, cases of corruption and other charges against ministers and deputies rarely reach the courts because the initiation of judicial proceedings in these cases requires authorization by parliament, which is usually precluded by strong party discipline. In 1998, an attempt to amend the constitution to remove parliamentary immunity in cases involving corruption failed to receive the necessary majority.

Finally, the weakness or absence of strong ties between political parties and civil society institutions (see Chapters 4 and 6) makes it difficult for even the mechanism of vertical accountability to operate meaningfully. The only open mechanism of such accountability is to the voters, who are limited to choosing one among equally oligarchical political parties.

Turkey today seems to occupy a secure place among the world's delegative democracies. There is little reason to fear that authoritarianism will return, but there is equally little reason to hope that democracy will soon become consolidated. As in many other delegative democracies, Turkish democracy may endure, but it may do so in a state of inherent vulnerability. As Larry Diamond reminds us, the mere persistence of democracy should not be confused "with the genuine stability that flows from consolidation. . . . Stability requires not merely a passive acceptance of the system, because there is no better alternative at the moment, but a positive belief in the moral value of democracy in principle."[5]

NOTES

1. Scott Mainwaring, "Party Systems in the Third Wave," *Journal of Democracy* 9 (July 1998): 69.

2. Guillermo O'Donnell, "Delegative Democracy," *Journal of Democracy* 5 (January 1994): 56, also 55–69.

3. In an interview in the Istanbul daily *Milliyet* on 13 June 1995, Prime Minister Çiller described how she had "worked for hours on my computer" and personally "determined even the finest details" of the economic policy package her government announced on 5 April 1994.

4. O'Donnell defines patronage as "the practice of securing jobs in the state bureaucracy for political allies and constituencies, with no or little consideration of the individual's merits or for whether the position is even necessary"—a practice widespread in Turkey. It is interesting that the term *accountability* has no direct equivalent in Turkish, Spanish, or Portuguese; "Transitions, Continuities, and Paradoxes," in Scott Mainwaring, Guillermo O'Donnell, and J. Samuel Valenzuela, eds., *Issues in Democratic Consolidation: The New South American Democracies in Comparative Perspective* (Notre Dame: University of Notre Dame Press, 1992), 38, 47.

5. Larry Diamond, "Democracy in Latin America: Degrees, Illusions, and Directions for Consolidation," in Tom Farer, ed., *Beyond Sovereignty: Collectively Defending Democracy in the Americas* (Baltimore: John Hopkins University Press, 1995), 76.

Abbreviations

AFU	Armed Forces Union
AP	Allianza Popular
BA	bureaucratic-authoritarian regime
DEP	Democracy Party
DISK	Confederation of Revolutionary Unions
DLP	Democratic Left Party
DP	Democratic Party
DTP	Democratic Turkey Party
ESG	Escola Superior de Guerra
FP	Freedom Party
GNA	Grand National Assembly
HEP	People's Labor Party
ISI	import substitution–based industrialization
JP	Justice Party
MP	Motherland Party
MÜSIAD	Independent Industrialists' and Businessmen's Association
NAP	Nationalist Action Party
NDP	Nationalist Democracy Party
NP	Nation Party

NSC	National Security Council
NSP	National Salvation Party
NTP	New Turkey Party
NUC	National Unity Committee
PDP	People's Democracy Party
PKK	Kurdistan Workers' Party
PP	Populist Party
RPNP	Republican Peasant Nation Party
RPP	Republican People's Party
RRP	Republican Reliance Party
SDP	Social Democratic Party
SDPP	Social Democratic Populist Party
TESK	Turkish Confederation of Small Traders and Artisans
TGNA	Turkish Grand National Assembly
TISK	Turkish Confederation of Employers Association
TLP	Turkish Labor Party
TOBB	Turkish Union of Chambers of Commerce, Industry, Maritime Trade, and Trade Exchange
TPP	True Path Party
Türk-Is	Confederation of Turkish Trade Unions
TÜSIAD	Turkish Industrialists' and Businessmen's Association
UCD	Central Democratic Union
UP	Unity Party
VP	Virtue Party
WP	Welfare Party

Bibliography

Acar, Feride. "The True Path Party, 1983–1989," in Metin Heper and Jacob M. Landau, eds., *Political Parties and Democracy in Turkey*. London: I. B. Tauris, 1991, 188–207.

Agüero, Felipe. "The Military and the Limits to Democratization in South America," in Scott Mainwaring, Guillermo O'Donnell, and J. Samuel Valenzuela, eds., *Issues in Democratic Consolidation: The New South American Democracies in Comparative Perspective*. Notre Dame: University of Notre Dame Press, 1992, 153–198.

Ahmad, Feroz. *The Turkish Experiment with Democracy, 1950–1975*. Boulder: Westview Press, 1977.

———. "The Political Economy of Kemalism," in Ali Kazancıgil and Ergun Özbudun, eds., *Atatürk: Founder of a Modern State*. London: C. Hurst, 1981, 145–163.

Alpay, Sahin, and Seyfettin Gürsel. *DSP-SHP: Nerede Birlesiyorlar, Nerede Ayrılıyorlar?* Istanbul: Afa, 1986.

Arat, Yesim. "Politics and Big Business: Janus-Faced Link to the State," in Metin Heper, ed., *Strong State and Economic Interest Groups: The Post-1980 Turkish Experience*. Berlin: Walter de Gruyter, 1991, 135–147.

Arcayürek, Cüneyt. *Demokrasinin Sonbaharı: 1977–1978*, Vol. 7. Ankara: Bilgi Yayınevi, 1985.

———. *Demokrasi Dur, 12 Eylül 1980: Nisan 1980–Eylül 1980*, Vol. 10. Ankara: Bilgi Yayınevi, 1986.

———. *Müdahalenin Ayak Sesleri: 1978–1979*, Vol. 8. Ankara: Bilgi Yayınevi, 1986.

————. *12 Eylüle Dogru Kosar Adım, Kasım 1979–Nisan 1980*, Vol. 9. Ankara: Bilgi Yayınevi, 1986.

Atatürk'ün Söylev ve Demeçleri, Vol. 2. Ankara: Türk Inkılap Tarihi Enstitüsü Yayınları, 1959, 275.

Ayata, Ayse. "Ideology, Social Bases, and Organizational Structure of the Post-1980 Political Parties," in Atila Eralp, Muharrem Tünay, and Birol Yesilada, eds., *The Political and Socioeconomic Transformation of Turkey*. Westport: Praeger, 1993, 31–49.

————. "The Emergence of Identity Politics in Turkey." *New Perspectives on Turkey* 17 (fall 1997): 59–73.

Ayata, Sencer. "Patronage, Party, and State: The Politicization of Islam in Turkey." *Middle East Journal* 50 (winter 1996): 40–56.

Barkey, Henri J. *The State and the Industrialization Crisis in Turkey*. Boulder: Westview Press, 1990.

Barkey, Henri J., and Graham E. Fuller. *Turkey's Kurdish Question*. Carnegie Commission on Preventing Deadly Conflict. Lanham: Rowman and Littlefield, 1998.

Bektas, Arsev. *Demokratiklesme Sürecinde Liderler Oligarsisi, CHP ve AP (1961–1980)*. Istanbul: Baglam, 1993.

Bianchi, Robert. *Interest Groups and Political Development in Turkey*. Princeton: Princeton University Press, 1984.

Birand, M. Ali. *12 Eylül Saat 04.00*. İstanbul: Karacan, 1984.

Bonime-Blanc, Andrea. *Spain's Transition to Democracy: The Politics of Constitution-Making*. Boulder: Westview Press, 1987.

Bugra, Ayse. "Class, Culture, and State: An Analysis of Interest Representation by Two Turkish Business Associations." *International Journal of Middle East Studies* 30 (November 1998): 521–539.

Burçak, Rıfkı Salim. *Türkiye'de Demokrasiye Geçis*. Istanbul: Olgaç Matbaası, 1979.

Burton, Michael, Richard Gunther, and John Higley. "Elites and Democratic Consolidation in Latin America and Southern Europe: An Overview," in John Higley and Richard Gunther, eds., *Elites and Democratic Consolidation in Latin America and Southern Europe*. Cambridge: Cambridge University Press, 1992, 323–348.

Çaglar, Bakır. "Anayasa Mahkemesi Kararlarında Demokrasi," in *Anayasa Yargısı*, Vol. 7. Ankara: Anayasa Mahkemesi Yayınları, 1990, 51–127.

Çakır, Rusen. *Ne Seriat, Ne Demokrasi: Refah Partisini Anlamak*. Istanbul: Metis, 1994.

Çalık, Mustafa. *Siyasî Kültür ve Sosyolojinin Bazı Kavramları Açısından MHP Hareketi: Kaynakları ve Gelisimi*. Ankara: Cedit, 1995.

Çınar, Menderes. "Rebuilding the Center: Mission Impossible?" *Private View* 1 (autumn 1997): 72–78.

Cizre-Sakallıoglu, Ümit. *AP-Ordu Iliskileri: Bir Ikilemin Anatomisi*. Istanbul: Iletisim Yayınları, 1993.

————. "Liberalism, Democracy and the Turkish Centre-Right: The Identity Crisis of the True Path Party." *Middle Eastern Studies* 32 (April 1996): 142–161.

Di Palma, Giuseppe. *To Craft Democracies: An Essay on Democratic Transitions*. Berkeley: University of California Press, 1990.

Diamond, Larry. "Rethinking Civil Society: Toward Democratic Consolidation." *Journal of Democracy* 5 (July 1994): 4–17.

————. "Democracy in Latin America: Degrees, Illusions, and Directions for Consolidation," in Tom Farer, ed., *Beyond Sovereignty: Collectively Defending Democracy in the Americas.* Baltimore: Johns Hopkins University Press, 1995, 52–104.

Duverger, Maurice. *Political Parties: Their Organization and Activity in the Modern State.* New York: Wiley, 1959.

Ergüder, Üstün. "The Motherland Party, 1983–1989," in Metin Heper and Jacob M. Landau, eds., *Political Parties and Democracy in Turkey.* London: I. B. Tauris, 1991, 152–169.

Ergüder, Üstün, and Richard I. Hofferbert. "The 1983 General Elections in Turkey: Continuity or Change in Voting Patterns?" in Metin Heper and Ahmet Evin, eds., *State, Democracy, and Military: Turkey in the 1980s.* Berlin: Walter de Gruyter, 1988, 81–102.

Erogul, Cem. *Demokrat Parti: Tarihi ve Ideolojisi.* Ankara: A. Ü. Siyasal Bilgiler Fakültesi Yayını, 1970.

Esmer, Yılmaz. "Manufacturing Industries: Giants with Hesitant Voices," in Metin Heper, ed., *Strong State and Economic Interest Groups: The Post-1980 Turkish Experience.* Berlin: Walter de Gruyter, 1991, 119–134.

————. "Parties and the Electorate: A Comparative Analysis of Voter Profiles of Turkish Political Parties," in Çigdem Balım et al., eds., *Turkey: Political, Social, and Economic Challenges in the 1990s.* Leiden: E. J. Brill, 1995, 74–89.

Evin, Ahmet. "Demilitarization and Civilianization of the Regime," in Metin Heper and Ahmet Evin, eds., *Politics in the Third Turkish Republic.* Boulder: Westview Press, 1994, 23–40.

Evren, Kenan. *Kenan Evren'in Anıları,* Vol. 1. Istanbul: Milliyet, 1990.

Frey, Frederick W. *The Turkish Political Elite.* Cambridge: MIT Press, 1965.

Gallagher, Michael. "Conclusion," in Michael Gallagher and Michael Marsh, eds., *Candidate Selection in Comparative Perspective: The Secret Garden of Politics.* London: Sage, 1988, 236–245.

Gologlu, Mahmut. *Demokrasiye Geçis: 1946–1950.* Istanbul: Kaynak Yayınları, 1982.

Hale, William. *Turkish Politics and the Military.* London: Routledge, 1994.

Heper, Metin. *The State Tradition in Turkey.* Walkington: Eothen, 1985.

————. "The Executive in the Third Turkish Republic, 1982–1989." *Governance* 3 (1990): 299–319.

————. "Interest-Group Politics in Post-1980 Turkey: Lingering Monism," in Metin Heper, ed., *Strong State and Economic Interest Groups: The Post-1980 Turkish Experience.* Berlin: Walter de Gruyter, 1991, 163–176.

————. "The State and Interest Groups with Special Reference to Turkey," in Metin Heper, ed., *Strong State and Economic Interest Groups: The Post-1980 Turkish Experience.* Berlin: Walter de Gruyter, 1991, 3–23.

————. "Strong State as a Problem for the Consolidation of Democracy: Turkey and Germany Compared." *Comparative Political Studies* 25 (July 1992): 169–194.

Heper, Metin, and Aylin Güney. "The Military and Democracy in the Third Turkish Republic." *Armed Forces and Society* 22 (summer 1996): 619–642.

Heper, Metin, and Aylin Güney-Avcı. "Military and the Consolidation of Democracy: The Recent Turkish Experience." Unpublished paper.

Huntington, Samuel P. "Will More Countries Become Democratic?" *Political Science Quarterly* 99 (summer 1984): 193–218.

————. *The Third Wave: Democratization in the Late Twentieth Century.* Norman: University of Oklahoma Press, 1991.

Inalcık, Halil. "The Nature of Traditional Society: Turkey," in Robert E. Ward and Dankwart A. Rustow, eds., *Political Modernization in Japan and Turkey.* Princeton: Princeton University Press, 1964, 42–63.

Inan, Nurkut, and Cüneyt Ozansoy. "Yasama Faaliyeti Açısından 12 Eylül," *Yapıt,* No. 14 (1986): 3–43.

Isleyen Rejim, *Isleyen Devlet.* Paper prepared by Necmettin Cevheri, member of the Central Executive Committee of the True Path Party. Ankara, 1991.

Kalaycıoglu, Ersin. "Commercial Groups: Love-Hate Relationship with the State," in Metin Heper, ed., *Strong State and Economic Interest Groups: The Post-1980 Turkish Experience.* Berlin: Walter de Gruyter, 1991, 79–87.

————. "Elections and Party Preferences in Turkey: Changes and Continuities in the 1990s." *Comparative Political Studies* 27 (October 1994): 402–424.

Karpat, Kemal. *Turkey's Politics: The Transition to a Multi-Party System.* Princeton: Princeton University Press, 1959.

Katz, Richard S., and Peter Mair. "Changing Models of Party Organization and Party Democracy: The Emergence of the Cartel Party." *Party Politics* 1 (January 1995): 5–28.

Landau, Jacob M. "The National Salvation Party in Turkey." *Asian and African Studies* 11, No. 1 (1976): 1–57.

————. "The Nationalist Action Party in Turkey." *Journal of Contemporary History* 17 (1982): 587–606.

Levi, Avner. "The Justice Party, 1961–1980," in Metin Heper and Jacob M. Landau, eds., *Political Parties and Democracy in Turkey.* London: I. B. Tauris, 1991, 134–151.

Lewis, Bernard. *The Emergence of Modern Turkey.* London: Oxford University Press, 1968.

Liebert, Ulrike, and Maurizio Cotta, eds. *Parliament and Democratic Consolidation in Southern Europe: Greece, Italy, Portugal, Spain, and Turkey.* London: Pinter, 1990.

Linz, Juan J. "An Authoritarian Regime: Spain," in Erik Allardt and Stein Rokkan, eds., *Mass Politics: Studies in Political Sociology.* New York: Free Press, 1970, 251–283.

————. "Totalitarian and Authoritarian Regimes," in Fred I. Greenstein and Nelson W. Polsby, eds., *Handbook of Political Science: Macropolitical Theory.* Reading, Mass.: Addison-Wesley, 1975, 175–411.

————. *The Breakdown of Democratic Regimes: Crisis, Breakdown, and Reequilibration.* Baltimore: Johns Hopkins University Press, 1978.

Linz, Juan, and Alfred Stepan. "Political Crafting of Democratic Consolidation or Destruction: European and South American Comparisons," in Robert A. Pastor, ed., *Democracy in the Americas: Stopping the Pendulum.* New York: Holmes and Meier, 1989, 41–61.

————. *Problems of Democratic Transition and Consolidation: Southern Europe, South America, and Post-Communist Europe.* Baltimore: Johns Hopkins University Press, 1996.

————, eds. *The Breakdown of Democratic Regimes.* Baltimore: Johns Hopkins University Press, 1978.

Mainwaring, Scott. "Transitions to Democracy and Democratic Consolidation: Theoretical and Comparative Issues," in Scott Mainwaring, Guillermo O'Donnell, and J. Samuel Valenzuela, eds., *Issues in Democratic Consolidation: The New South American Democracies in Comparative Perspective.* Notre Dame: University of Notre Dame Press, 1992, 294–341.

————. "Party Systems in the Third Wave." *Journal of Democracy* 9 (July 1998): 67–81.

Mainwaring, Scott, and Donald Share. "Transitions Through Transaction: Democratization in Brazil and Spain," in W. A. Selcher, ed., *Political Liberalization in Brazil: Dynamics, Dilemmas, and Future Prospects.* Boulder: Westview Press, 1986, 175–215.

Mango, Andrew. "The Social Democratic Populist Party, 1983–1989," in Metin Heper and Jacob M. Landau, eds., *Political Parties and Democracy in Turkey.* London: I. B. Tauris, 1991, 170–187.

Maravall, Jose Maria, and Julian Santamaria. "Political Change in Spain and the Prospects for Democracy," in Guillermo O'Donnell, Philippe C. Schmitter, and Laurence Whitehead, eds., *Transitions from Authoritarian Rule: Southern Europe.* Baltimore: Johns Hopkins University Press, 1986, 71–108.

Mardin, Serif. "Power, Civil Society and Culture in the Ottoman Empire." *Comparative Studies in Society and History* 11 (June 1969): 258–281.

————. "Center-Periphery Relations: A Key to Turkish Politics." *Deadalus* (winter 1972): 169–190.

————. "Religion and Secularism in Turkey," in Ali Kazancıgil and Ergun Özbudun, eds., *Atatürk: Founder of a Modern State.* London: C. Hurst, 1981, 191–219.

Moore, Clement H. "The Single Party as a Source of Legitimacy," in Samuel P. Huntington and Clement H. Moore, eds., *Authoritarian Politics in Modern Society: The Dynamics of Established One-Party Systems.* New York: Basic Books, 1970, 48–72.

Morlino, Leonardo. "Political Parties and Democratic Consolidation in Southern Europe," in Richard Gunther, P. Nikiforos Diamandouros, and Hans-Jürgen Puhle, eds., *The Politics of Democratic Consolidation: Southern Europe in Comparative Perspective.* Baltimore: Johns Hopkins University Press, 1995, 315–388.

National Security Council, Turkey. *12 September in Turkey: Before and After.* Ankara: General Secretariat of the National Security Council, 1982.

Neumann, Sigmund. "Toward a Comparative Study of Political Parties," in Sigmund Neumann, ed., *Modern Political Parties: Approaches to Comparative Politics.* Chicago: University of Chicago Press, 1956, 395–421.

O'Donnell, Guillermo. *Modernization and Bureaucratic-Authoritarianism: Studies in South American Politics.* Berkeley: Institute of International Studies, University of California, 1973.

————. "Tensions in the Bureaucratic-Authoritarian State and the Question of Democracy," in David Collier, ed., *The New Authoritarianism in Latin America.* Princeton: Princeton University Press, 1979, 285–318.

————. "Transitions, Continuities, and Paradoxes," in Scott Mainwaring, Guillermo O'Donnell, and J. Samuel Valenzuela, eds., *Issues in*

Democratic Consolidation: The New South American Democracies in Comparative Perspective. Notre Dame: University of Notre Dame Press, 1992, 16–56.

———. "Delegative Democracy." *Journal of Democracy* 5 (January 1994): 55–69.

Okyar, Fethi. *Üç Devirde Bir Adam.* Istanbul: Tercüman Yayınları, 1980.

Önis, Ziya. "Political Economy of Turkey in the 1980s: Anatomy of Unorthodox Liberalism," in Metin Heper, ed., *Strong State and Economic Interest Groups: The Post-1980 Turkish Experience.* Berlin: Walter de Gruyter, 1991, 27–40.

———. "The Political Economy of Islamic Resurgence in Turkey: The Rise of the Welfare Party in Perspective." *Third World Quarterly* 18, No. 4 (1997): 743–766.

Özbudun, Ergun. "Established Revolution Versus Unfinished Revolution: Contrasting Patterns of Democratization in Mexico and Turkey," in Samuel P. Huntington and Clement H. Moore, eds., *Authoritarian Politics in Modern Society: The Dynamics of Established One-Party Systems.* New York: Basic Books, 1970, 380–405.

———. *Social Change and Political Participation in Turkey.* Princeton: Princeton University Press, 1976.

———. "The Turkish Party System: Institutionalization, Polarization, and Fragmentation." *Middle Eastern Studies* 17 (April 1981): 228–240.

———. "Islam and Politics in Modern Turkey: The Case of the National Salvation Party," in Barbara Freyer Stowasser, ed., *The Islamic Impulse.* London: Croom Helm, 1987, 142–156.

———. "Turkey: Crises, Interruptions, and Reequilibrations," in Larry Diamond, Juan J. Linz, and Seymour Martin Lipset, eds., *Politics in Developing Countries: Comparing Experiences with Democracy.* Boulder: Lynne Rienner, 1990, 175–217.

———. "The Post-1980 Legal Framework for Interest Group Associations," in Metin Heper, ed., *Strong State and Economic Interest Groups: The Post-1980 Turkish Experience.* Berlin: Walter de Gruyter, 1991, 41–53.

———. "State Elites and Democratic Political Culture in Turkey," in Larry Diamond, ed., *Political Culture and Democracy in Developing Countries.* Boulder: Lynne Rienner, 1993, 247–268.

———. *Türk Anayasa Hukuku.* Ankara: Yetkin Yayınları, 1993.

———. "The Ottoman Legacy and the Middle East State Tradition," in L. Carl Brown, ed., *Imperial Legacy: The Ottoman Imprint on the Balkans and the Middle East.* New York: Columbia University Press, 1996, 133–157.

Pasquino, Gianfranco. "The Demise of the First Fascist Regime and Italy's Transition to Democracy: 1943–1948," in Guillermo O'Donnell, Philippe C. Schmitter, and Laurence Whitehead, eds., *Transitions from Authoritarian Rule: Southern Europe.* Baltimore: Johns Hopkins University Press, 1986, 45–70.

PIAR (Piyasa Arastirmalari Merkezi). "Siyasal Islanın Ayak Sesleri." Unpublished paper, 1997.

Przeworski, Adam. *Democracy and the Market: Political and Economic Reforms in Eastern Europe and Latin America.* Cambridge: Cambridge University Press, 1991.

Przeworski, Adam, Michael Alvarez, José Antonio Cheibub, and Fernando Limogni. "What Makes Democracies Endure?" *Journal of Democracy* 7 (January 1996): 39–55.

Rae, Douglas W. *The Political Consequences of Electoral Laws.* New Haven: Yale University Press, 1967.

Rustow, Dankwart A. "Atatürk as Founder of a State," in *Prof. Dr. Yavuz Abadan'a Armagan.* Ankara: A. Ü. Siyasal Bilgiler Fakültesi Yayını, 1969, 517–573.

————. "Transitions to Democracy: Toward a Dynamic Model." *Comparative Politics* 2 (April 1970): 337–363.

Sarıbay, Ali Yasar. *Türkiye'de Modernlesme, Din ve Parti Politikası: MSP Örnek Olayı.* Istanbul: Alan, 1985.

Sartori, Giovanni. *Parties and Party Systems: A Framework for Analysis.* Cambridge: Cambridge University Press, 1976.

Sayarı, Sabri. "Some Notes on the Beginnings of Mass Political Participation in Turkey," in Engin D. Akarlı with Gabriel Ben-Dor, eds., *Political Participation in Turkey: Historical Background and Present Problems.* Istanbul: Bogaziçi University Publications, 1975, 121–133.

————. "Aspects of Party Organization in Turkey." *Middle East Journal* 30 (spring 1976): 187–199.

Schmitter, Philippe C. "Still the Century of Corporatism?" in Philippe C. Schmitter and Gerhard Lembruch, eds., *Trends Toward Corporatist Intermediation.* Beverly Hills: Sage, 1979, 7–52.

Schneider, William. "Electoral Behavior and Political Development." Mimeo, Harvard University, Center for International Affairs, 1972.

Schattschneider, E. E. *Party Government.* New York: Holt, Rinehart, and Winston, 1942.

Sen, Serdar. *Refah Partisinin Teori ve Pratigi.* Istanbul: Sarmal, 1995.

Stepan, Alfred. *The Military in Politics: Changing Patterns in Brazil.* Princeton: Princeton University Press, 1974.

————. "Paths Toward Redemocratization: Theoretical and Comparative Considerations," in Guillermo O'Donnell, Philippe C. Schmitter, and Laurence Whitehead, eds., *Transitions from Authoritarian Rule: Comparative Perspectives.* Baltimore: Johns Hopkins University Press, 1986, 65–84.

————. *Rethinking Military Politics: Brazil and the Southern Cone.* Princeton: Princeton University Press, 1988.

Stirling, Paul. *Turkish Village.* New York: Wiley, 1965.

Sunar, Ilkay. *State and Society in the Politics of Turkey's Development.* Ankara: A. Ü. Siyasal Bilgiler Fakültesi Yayını, 1974.

————. "State, Society, and Democracy in Turkey," in Wojtech Mastny and R. Craig Nation, eds., *Turkey Between East and West: New Challenges for a Rising Regional Power.* Boulder: Westview Press, 1996, 141–154.

Tachau, Frank. "The Republican People's Party, 1945–1980," in Metin Heper and Jacob M. Landau, eds., *Political Parties and Democracy in Turkey.* London: I. B. Tauris, 1991, 99–118.

Tanör, Bülent. *Iki Anayasa, 1961–1982.* Istanbul: Beta, 1986.

Timur, Taner. *Türk Devrimi: Tarihi Anlamı ve Felsefi Temeli.* Ankara: A. Ü. Siyasal Bilgiler Fakültesi Yayını, 1968.

Toker, Metin. *Demokrasimizin Ismet Pasa'lı Yılları: Tek Partiden Çok Partiye,* *1944–1950.* Ankara: Bilgi Yayınevi, 1990.
————. *Demokrasimizin Ismet Pasa'lı Yılları: Demokrasiden Darbeye,* *1957–1960.* Ankara: Bilgi Yayınevi, 1991.
————. *Demokrasimizin Ismet Pasa'lı Yılları: DP Yokus Asagı, 1954–1957.* Ankara: Bilgi Yayınevi, 1991.
————. *Demokrasimizin Ismet Pasa'lı Yılları: Yarı Silahlı, Yarı Külahlı Bir Ara* *Rejim, 1960–1961.* Ankara: Bilgi Yayınevi, 1991.
————. *Demokrasimizin Ismet Pasa'lı Yılları: Ismet Pasa'nın Son Yılları,* *1965–1973.* Ankara: Bilgi Yayınevi, 1993.
Toprak, Binnaz. *Islam and Political Development in Turkey.* Leiden: E. J. Brill, 1981.
Turan, Ilter. "Stages of Political Development in the Turkish Republic," in Ergun Özbudun, ed., *Perspectives on Democracy in Turkey.* Ankara: Turkish Political Science Association, 1988, 59–112.
Türsan, Huri. "Pernicious Party Factionalism as a Constant of Transitions to Democracy in Turkey." *Democratization* 2 (spring 1995): 169–184.
TÜSES (Türkiye Sosyal Ekonomik Siyasal Arastirmalar Vakfi) Veri Arastırma A. S. *Türkiye'de Siyasi, Parti Seçmenlerinin Nitelikleri,* *Kimlikleri ve Egilimleri.* Ankara: TÜSES, 1996.
TÜSIAD. *Türk Toplumunun Degerleri.* Istanbul: TÜSIAD, 1991.
Ugur, Aydın. "Batıda ve Türkiye'de Sivil Toplum: Kavram ve Olgunun Gelisim Serüveni," in *75 Yılda Tebaa'dan Yurttasa Dogru.* Istanbul: Tarih Vakfı Yayınları, 1998, 213–226.
Valenzuela, J. Samuel. "Democratic Consolidation in Post-Transitional Settings: Notion, Process, and Facilitating Conditions," in Scott Mainwaring, Guillermo O'Donnell, and J. Samuel Valenzuela, eds., *Issues in Democratic Consolidation: The New South American* *Democracies in Comparative Perspective.* Notre Dame: University of Notre Dame Press, 1992, 57–104.
Von Beyme, Klaus. "Party Leadership and Change in Party Systems: Towards a Postmodern Party State." *Government and Opposition* 31 (spring 1996): 135–159.
Weisman, Carlos H. *Reversal of Development in Argentina.* Princeton: Princeton University Press, 1987.
Yetkin, Çetin. *Türkiye'de Tek Parti Yönetimi, 1930–1945.* Istanbul: Altın Kitaplar Yayınevi, 1983.
Yılmaz, Hakan. "Democratization from Above in Response to the International Context: Turkey, 1945–1950." *New Perspectives on Turkey* 17 (fall 1997): 1–37.
Yücekök, Ahmet N. *Siyaset Sosyolojisi Açısından Türkiye'de Parlamentonun* *Evrimi.* Ankara: A. Ü. Siyasal Bilgiler Fakültesi Yayını, 1983.

Index

About the Book

Turkey offers a rich laboratory for comparativists interested in issues of democratization and democratic consolidation: since 1945, it has witnessed no fewer than three breakdowns of the democratic process (1960, 1971, 1980) and three retransitions to democracy (1961, 1973, 1983). Özbudun analyzes a half century of Turkish politics, focusing on the country's experiences with democracy and providing a theoretical and comparative perspective.

Among the challenges to democratic consolidation Turkey faces are the guarantees that departing military governments extracted as a price of relinquishing power; the volatility and fragmentation of the Turkish party system; the rise of political Islam; and the Kurdish separatist movement. As a result of these and other challenges, argues Özbudun, although there is little reason to fear that authoritarianism will return, there is every reason to assume that Turkey will remain for some time, to use Guillermo O'Donnell's term, only a delegative democracy.

Ergun Özbudun is professor of political science at Bilkent University (Turkey) and vice president of the Turkish Democracy Foundation. Previously, he was professor and chair of constitutional law and comparative politics at the Ankara University School of Law. His many publications include *Party Cohesion in Western Democracies, Social Change and Political Participation in Turkey,* (as editor) *Electoral Politics in the Middle East,* and (as editor) *Competitive Elections in Developing Countries.*